Quilted Diamonds 2

more Austen-tatious diamonds to hand piece

Linda Franz

Copyright Statement from the Author

The book and DVD are intended to educate and entertain you. If you enjoy this book and the DVD lesson, please tell your friends, and invite them to visit www.lindafranz.com

You will want to share your enjoyment of the hand piecing technique with your friends, but it is a violation of copyright to make copies of the patterns or the instructions in the book or on DVD, whether or not you profit from it.

The DVD is for home use only, and all other rights are expressly reserved. It is strictly prohibited to copy the DVD or show the DVD in public, whether for profit or not.

Teachers and quilt shop owners are welcome to use the DVD and the instructions in the book in their classes, if every student purchases *Quilted Diamonds 2*. Otherwise, please contact me. I am happy to grant written permission for use which you can display to the quilters so they will know you are not violating copyright. Use without written permission is a violation of copyright.

Thank you for respecting the time, effort and investment I have made in presenting my lesson to you in this way.

"It was a plan to promote the happiness of all."[1]

National Library of Canada Cataloguing in Publication

Franz, Linda

 Quilted diamonds 2 : more Austen-tatious diamonds to hand

piece / Linda Franz.

Accompanied by a DVD.

Includes bibliographical references and index.

ISBN 0-9730304-2-9

 1. Quilting--Patterns. 2. Austen, Jane, 1775-1817. I. Title.

TT835.F752 2004   746.46'041   C2004-900943-5

Published by
Linda Franz
2040 Watson Drive
Burlington Ontario
Canada L7R 3X4

For additional copies, please visit
www.lindafranz.com

First Printing March 2004

Printed in Canada

*It is
of all subjects
my delight.*[2]

contents

menu on DVD

You can play the entire lesson from the beginning or select individual scenes from the menu.

introduction
preparation
  fabric
  making templates
  ironing the templates
  rotary cutting
  marking seam lines
  sewing kits

sewing basics
  needles
  thread
  threading the needle
  sewing sequence
  mirror image
  quilter's knot

hand stitching
  pinning
  running stitch
  ¼ inch seams
  seam endings
  crossing seams
  inset seams
  many seams converging
  curves
  adding matches

pressing & trimming
using Electric Quilt
advantages of hand piecing
credits

introduction

Hand piecing is an uncomplicated pleasure; making a DVD is a complicated one!

My dear friend, Mary Althaus, taught me how to hand piece with freezer paper templates in January 1998, and it changed everything about quilting for me. This book is my way of sharing the pleasure with you.

Quilted Diamonds 2 is a different kind of quilt book.

To fulfill my dream for this book about quilting by hand, I relied on some sophisticated technology. My goal was to actually demonstrate the advantages of hand piecing with freezer paper templates and to share my enjoyment of hand sewing with you. The 101 new diamond designs may catch your eye in the first place, and then I hope that the relaxing technique will feel as good in your hands as it does in mine.

Quilted Diamonds 2 is the first quilt book to be published with the lesson on DVD.

As far as I know, no other quilt book includes a lesson almost two hours long on DVD, for the price of a book alone.

A picture is worth a thousand words—and there are several hundred pictures in this book—but a moving picture is worth even more.

When I started on this adventure in film making I did not know how complicated it would be to present a lesson in this way.

Writing the script and preparing the demonstrations took several months and the crew spent more than 24 hours at our house filming the main "shoot"—for which I had estimated 8 hours. That is one lesson I learned about show biz—take a generous estimate and multiply by three!

Making the DVD was very hard work but it was fun too. The director of photography, Robbi Hinds CSC, climbed to heights to capture the "action."

There were many long days in the editing studio plus sessions of additional photography, spread over several weeks, before the DVD could be "mastered."

Michael Lennick, our talented director, suggested that making a movie is similar to making a quilt—creating special pieces and then stitching them together.

Making quilts is more relaxing than making movies, but I would not have missed this experience for the world! I hope you will approve of the hand piecing movie that Michael and I "quilted" together for you.

Quilted Diamonds 2 emphasizes the advantages and simplicity of a technique, rather than a few projects.

Many quilters are initially attracted to hand piecing because it is portable and they soon fall in love with the relaxing, comfortable motion of making a simple running stitch. Piecing by hand is just as enjoyable as quilting by hand, but easier to take along. Hand piecers can sew in found time, on the go, or with friends.

Emily's mother hand pieces while Emily does her schoolwork. Emily drew this for Monkey.

Hand piecing is portable, so you can do it while you spend time with your children, watch TV with your husband, or visit with patients in a nursing home. It is nice to have a headset on the phone too. You can hand piece when you cannot sew on the machine. The benefits of portability are easy to understand!

In *Quilted Diamonds 2*, the emphasis is on the advantages and simplicity of the process. There is variety in the diamond patterns in this book and in my first book, *Quilted Diamonds: Jane Austen, Jane Stickle & Friends*, but the technique for all of them is the same. The stitching is reassuringly repetitive and the method is the same for straight seams, curves, insets, and pieces of any shape and size.

The technique in *Quilted Diamonds 2* applies in a wide variety of designs.

The technique employs freezer paper templates in the finished size and requires the seam line to be drawn in pencil on the wrong side of the fabric.

Freezer paper templates are perfect for this technique. They are adaptable for any design and can be used over and over again.

Also, having seam lines and crosshairs marked on the fabric simplifies the process and makes it more accurate. Just line up two pieces, right sides together, and sew with a running stitch from crosshair to crosshair, backstitching every time you load the needle, or about every ½ inch. It is simple enough for a child and challenging enough for an accomplished quilter.

The crosshairs at the end of each seam make it easy to pin and stitch accurately, even when the pieces are oddly shaped, so this approach promotes "continuous" stitching—where one seam follows easily upon the last without breaking the thread.

By providing close-up how-to photos in the book, plus the stitching on the DVD, I hope to give you confidence to try any design, whether the pieces in your blocks are squares, diamonds, triangles, or curves, and whether they are large or small.

Another benefit of templates is that it applies both to individual quilt blocks and to layouts or settings. Since freezer paper templates are the finished size, you do not need to consider the seam allowances until you are cutting the fabric. The same approach works whether I am drawing one quilt block, an entire bed quilt or the front of a blouse. "If I can draw it, I can cut it apart and sew it together." That is design freedom!

The diamonds in Love & Friendship (1999-2000) are easier than they look. Everything is accomplished with a simple running stitch.

Almost all of the quilt was pieced away from home, often while traveling in the car to and from the nursing home where my father lived.

The setting was inspired by a diamond medallion quilt made by Jane Austen, her sister and their mother, in about 1812. Altogether it has more than 5800 pieces.

The patterns for these 209 diamonds are in my first book, *Quilted Diamonds: Jane Austen, Jane Stickle & Friends.*

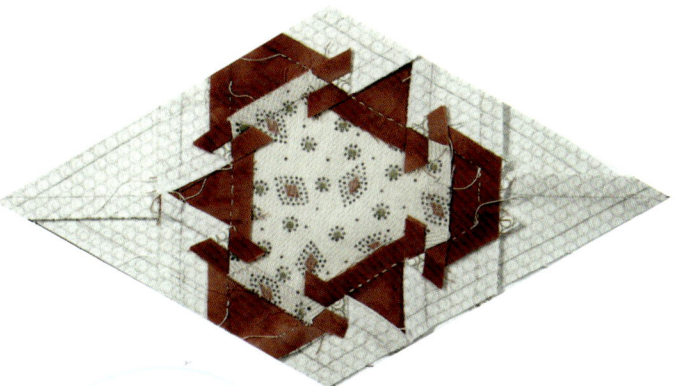

Every pattern in *Quilted Diamonds 2* was photographed from the wrong side.

Quilted Diamonds 2 blends computer age technology with age-old handcraft, with the optional CD.

Complex designs are often easier by hand than by machine, so hand piecing can be especially suited to quilters who get carried away designing on the computer!

When I 'staggered' and 'partitioned' my way to creating diamond #4, *"She stepped boldly forward, carelessly humming a tune,"* in Electric Quilt, I could hardly wait to cut all those little pieces apart and sew them together—by hand.

Every diamond pattern is shown in three variations in *Quilted Diamonds 2*.

My first two hand pieced bed quilts are both blue and white. I started making two-fabric quilts because it was easier than hauling my stash to and from Florida every winter and because I like these colors for decorating. Friends take delight in teasing me about only using blue, so please notice that each pattern in the book is shown in three fabric combinations with 2, 3, 4 or more fabrics in each diamond.

Some quilters are surprised—and intimidated—by the many choices for pressing hand pieced blocks. In 1999, when I first started sharing my quilting tips online, I began photographing the back of my finished blocks to show how they were pressed. By showing one example of pressing for each diamond, I hope to take some of the mystery out of it for you. Pressing in a radiating manner is one of my favorite advantages of hand piecing. It makes hand pieced blocks look their best and makes the quilting easier.

Every pattern also includes markings for suggested grain line and a diagram with suggested sewing sequence, which was also a popular feature of my first book.

Quilted Diamonds 2 includes detailed step-by-step photos and ideas for settings.

Even without the lesson on DVD, quilters will find everything they need to know in the detailed step-by-step photographs and ideas for settings. There is even a photo with a comment or tip at the bottom of each pattern page—for extra measure!

As you can see, this book is different in several ways. I *"stepped boldly forward, carelessly humming a tune,"* and *Quilted Diamonds 2* fulfills my personal dream as a quilter and teacher.

When you have had time to think it all over, I hope you will be satisfied with what I have done.[3] I would like to think that the DVD and the book will bring you some of the pleasure that Mary's hand piecing lesson brought to me, and that you will enjoy this simple, relaxing method of turning fabric into diamonds.

Linda

Ah ha! Proof that I have fabrics that are 'not blue' in my stash!

Jane Austen

A baby girl was born in December 1775 in rural England, the seventh child and second daughter of the rector of the parish. The little girl grew up devoted to her sister. One sister liked to draw pictures and the other liked to write stories. Neither of the girls ever married and they lived at home with their parents. The younger daughter, Jane, died in the summer of 1817. She would have been 42 on her next birthday. It was a brief life, with no extraordinary events, except that the little girl was Jane Austen, and her stories are masterpieces.

Jane Austen only wrote six novels but they have remained in print for almost 200 years. Praise for her writing knows no bounds and her popularity has never been greater than it is today. Even with every modern advantage, and her examples before them, modern novelists struggle to reach her high standard, and fail.

Dining parlor in Chawton

The novels were written on the tiny table in the dining parlor and are so perfectly crafted that it is almost impossible to analyze them. Change one scene, one character, and the entire structure falls apart. The more I read Jane Austen's novels, the more I marvel at her achievement. It is astounding to think that a young woman in her situation in life could create these literary masterpieces, listed on page 143. I am not alone in this sense of awe.

She is compared to Shakespeare and studied by academics all over the world. This paragon of classic literature sounds very intimidating, doesn't she? Her tales are moral and reflect a robust sense of right and wrong, but they are also *"light, bright, and sparkling"*[4] and understandable to each of us. She helps us know ourselves better—and she makes us laugh! Her special brilliance is in her humor and good natured fun.

Jane Austen is one of the best loved authors of all time and she was also well loved as a sister and an aunt. She had a happy home life. She was pretty, tall, graceful and danced well.

She enjoyed needlework and had beautiful hand writing. That is one reason I used the "Bickham" script in both of my books. It is based on the lettering of 18th century writing masters.

In about 1811, Jane, Cassandra and their mother made a pretty quilt (opposite page), with diamond shaped blocks. It is an unquilted coverlet, 97 x 105 inches, with diamonds in a medallion setting. The diamonds have sashing and there is a deep border of small diamonds. I took this photo of the quilt in Jane's bedroom at the Jane Austen Museum in Chawton and received permission from the owner to use this picture in the book, through the Jane Austen Memorial Trust.

Jane's bedroom in Chawton

I saw the quilt on visits to England before I was a quilter and eventually it inspired me to make a quilt with diamond shaped blocks, adapted from traditional square quilt blocks.

In *Quilted Diamonds: Jane Austen, Jane Stickle & Friends* and *Quilted Diamonds 2: more Austen-tatious diamonds to hand piece*, every diamond is named with phrases and situations from Jane Austen's novels.

When you choose your diamonds, it is my hope that the quotations will make you curious to know more about Elizabeth, Emma, Fanny and the other heroines, and entice you into reading—or re-reading—Jane Austen's enduring stories.

Dedication   To Russell Bays, my hero

Acknowledgments

Mary Althaus, for being a wonderful friend and for teaching me to hand piece.

Alison Murchie, dear sister, friend and beginning quilter, for her encouragement and for making a diamond for me!

Michael Lennick, director and friend, for his extraordinary patience and skill in recording my hand piecing lesson on DVD. It was our good fortune to work with such a talented producer, writer and director. His thirteen-part documentary "Rocket Science" for The Discovery Channel won Best Direction in a Documentary Series at the 2003 Houston International Film Festival, and he has many other impressive credits.

Donna Lucas, advisor and friend, for her encouragement, for introducing me to Michael, for her suggestions for the book cover and design, and for our long discussions about color, software and editing.

Penny McMorris of Electric Quilt for her kind assistance with the *QD2 CD.*

Karen and Emily Harrison for their interest in hand piecing, and the drawing of monkeys for Monkey.

Claire Baker for her gracious permission to use the photo of her diamond Quilt, "Jane in the Sky with Diamonds."

Sandy Arbuthnot, "Dowess" and online friend, for encouraging diamond makers by starting the Diamond of the Week (DOW) Challenge.

All of the friends who made diamonds and contributed to the special Friendship Quilt on page 142.

The kind and generous online friends who encouraged me to continue my hand piecing journey, especially Tilde Binger, Del Hersey, Lee Keyser, Dana Lynch, Jeanne Meddaugh, Roswitha Meidl, Judy Miller, Jeane Tucker, Emily Undem and Denise Werner, to name just a few. Many friends will recognize fabrics we traded and other tokens of friendship in the book and on the DVD. I was thinking of you!

Mr. Tom Carpenter, Trustee of the Jane Austen Memorial Trust, for his assistance in obtaining the kind permission of the owner of the Jane Austen Quilt to include my photograph of it in the book and DVD.

The Bennington Museum in Bennington Vermont, for their permission to use the poster of the Jane Stickle Quilt on the DVD.

1

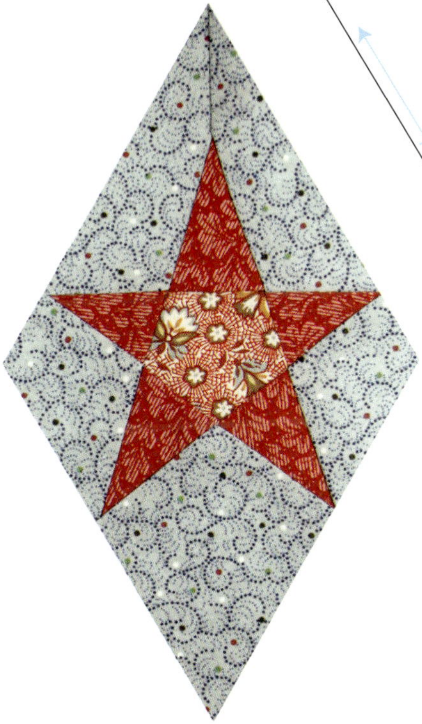

Miss Elizabeth's Star

Miss Elizabeth Bennet of *Pride and Prejudice* is probably the best loved of all Jane Austen's heroines.
Jane Austen referred to her as *the most delightful creature ever to appear in print.*[5] The slightly off-kilter lines
represent Elizabeth's independent spirit and her willingness to think for herself.

The entire diamond can be stitched continuously by turning a corner at the end of every seam without breaking the thread, as shown here.

There is one inset seam and there are some 'crooked' seams which you may choose to straighten when you are tracing. See the photos on pages 112 to 125 and the DVD lesson.

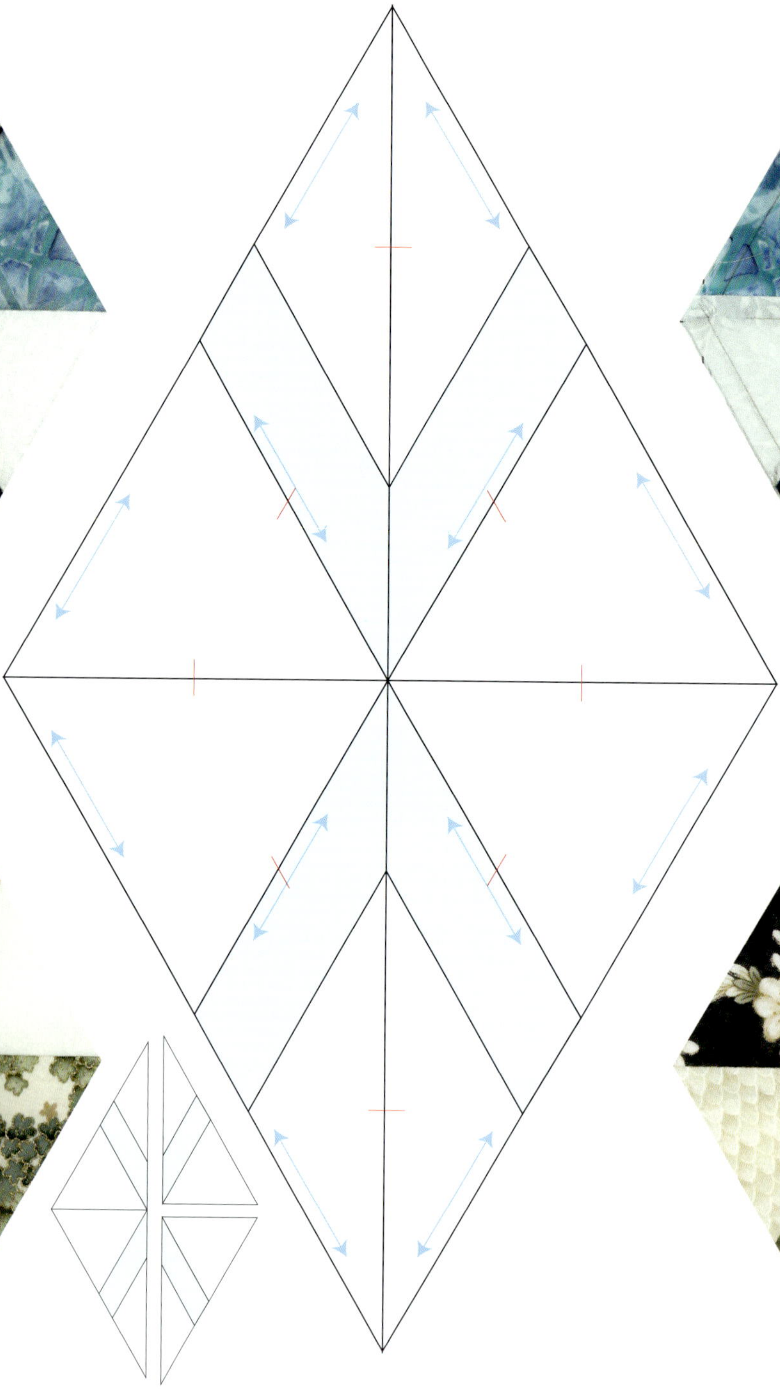

2

Enough for the happiness of the present hour.

(E Ch 26) To be in company, nicely dressed herself and seeing others nicely dressed, to sit and smile and look pretty, and say nothing, was enough for the happiness of the present hour. Harriet is contented to be at the Coles's party, in the midst of the pangs of disappointed affection.

This diamond has many seams converging in the middle and is demonstrated on the DVD. This diamond will lie flat!

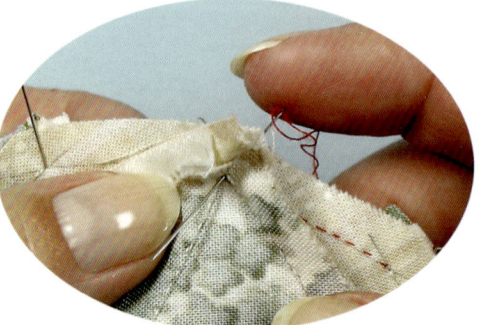

"Circle the intersection" to avoid having a tiny hole in the middle and press the seams in a radiating manner. See page 123.

Quilted Diamonds 2

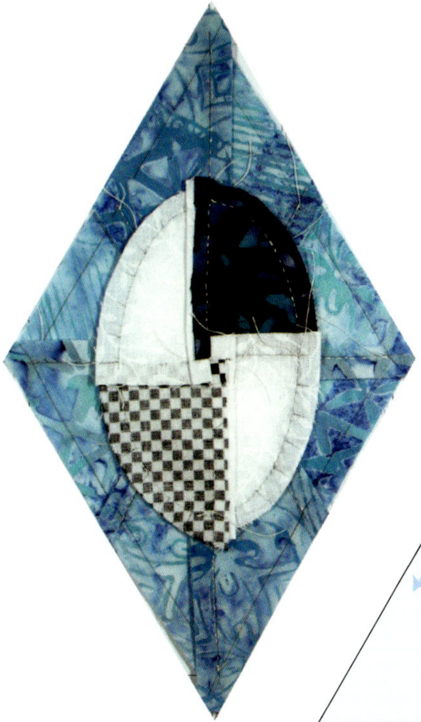

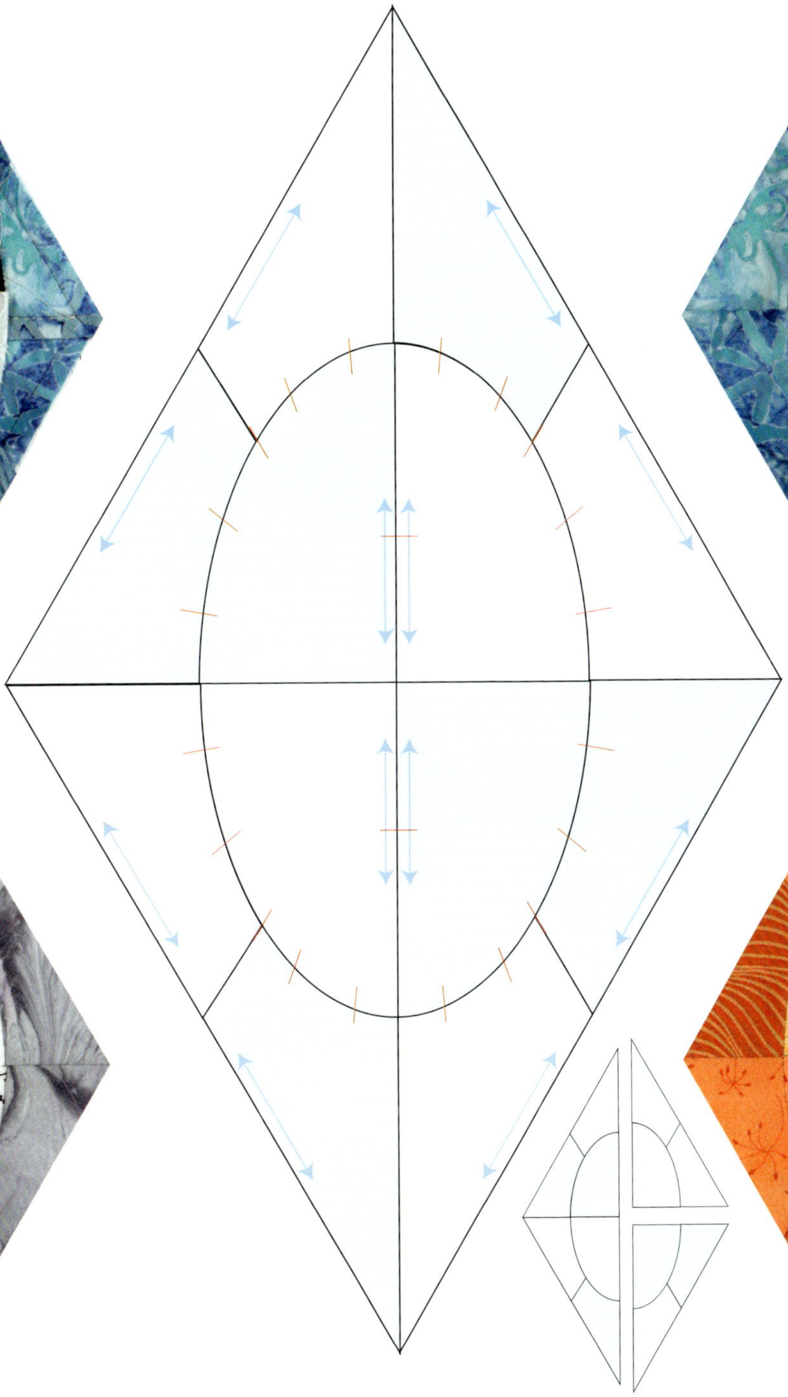

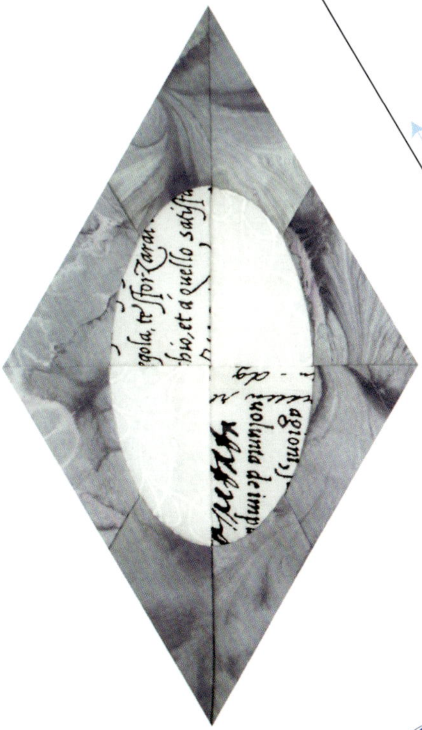

3

A new source of felicity arose to her.

(NA Ch 10) She had never taken a country walk since her arrival in Bath.
Will Catherine walk with Miss Tilney?

Many quilters find curved seams easier by hand than by machine. Mark matches before you cut the freezer paper pattern apart and pin one match at a time.

This is the time for your smallest stitches. Take one or two stitches at a time, instead of your normal load and backstitch every ½ inch or so. See pages 123-124.

Linda Franz

4

She stepped boldly forward, carelessly humming a tune.

(NA Ch 21) How glad I am that Northanger is what it is! If it had been like some other places,
I do not know that, in such a night as this, I could have answered for my courage...
Catherine's heart beat quick, but her courage did not fail her.

Very small interior ✳ pieces like
these do not need to be on straight
grain. This makes it faster to cut
out. See page 123 and the DVD for
more about curved seams.

You can join all of the small
triangles continuously, without
breaking the thread. This diamond
is easier than it looks.

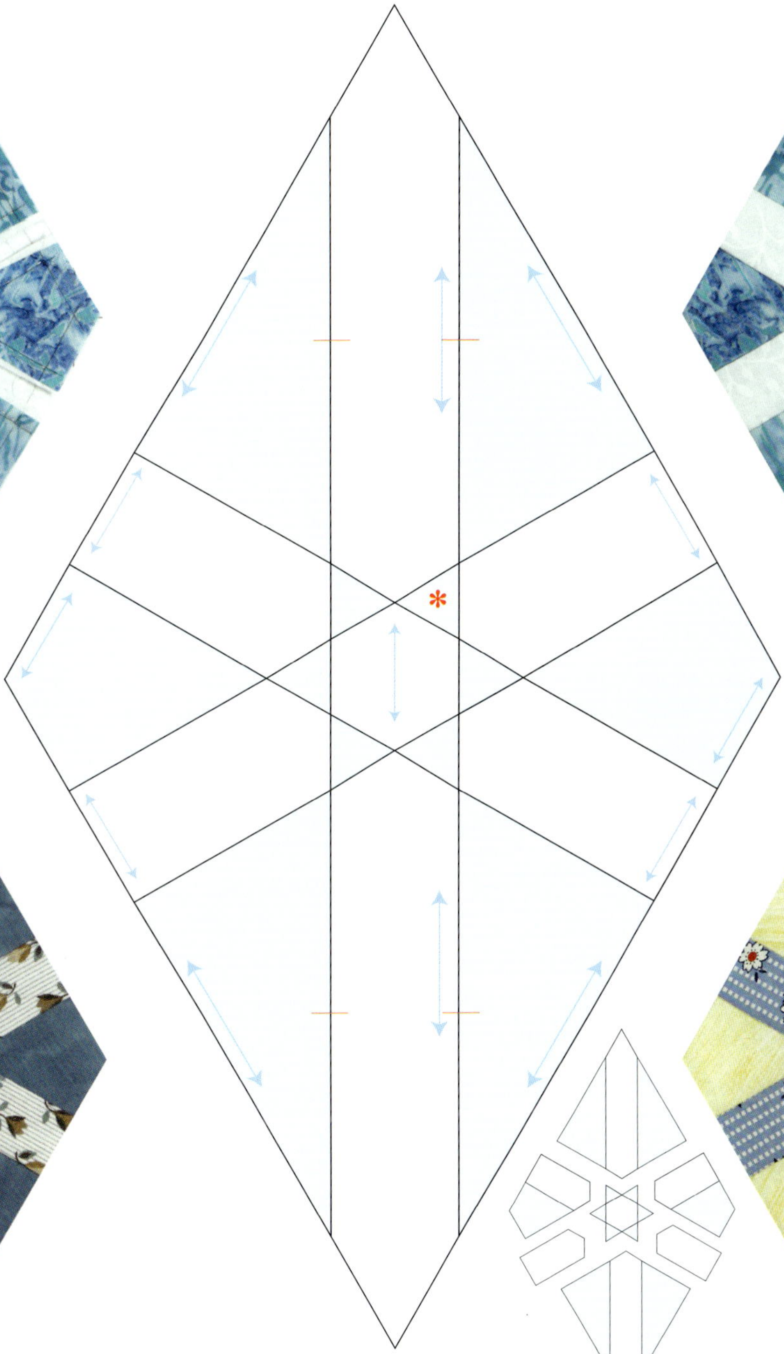

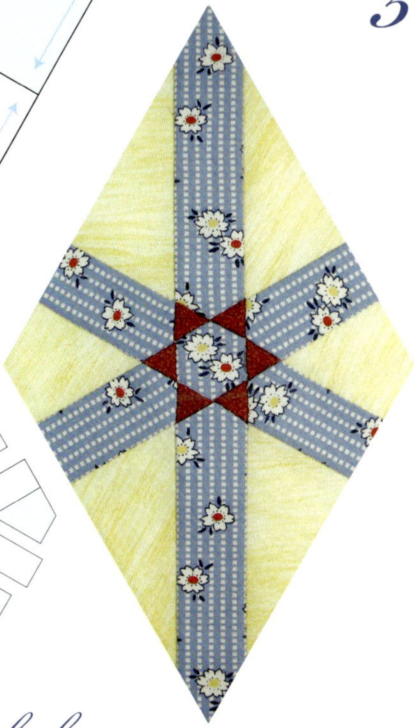

5

A pleasant drive home by moonlight.

(MP Ch 6) *Why should not we make a little party?* The Bertrams and Crawfords plan to travel from Mansfield to Sotherton *and have a pleasant drive home by moonlight.*

Very small interior * pieces like these do not need to be on straight grain. Steady them with a toothpick to keep your fingers away from a hot iron. Don't worry! They look bigger

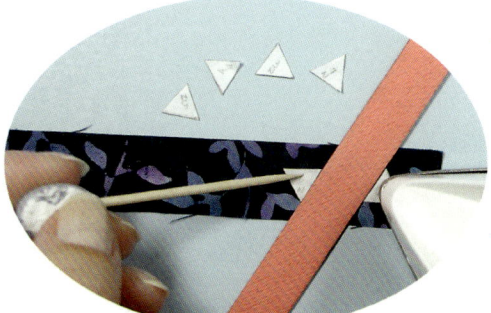

with the seam allowance and you can join all of the small triangles to the hexagon without breaking the thread, as on page 122 and in the DVD lesson for inset seams.

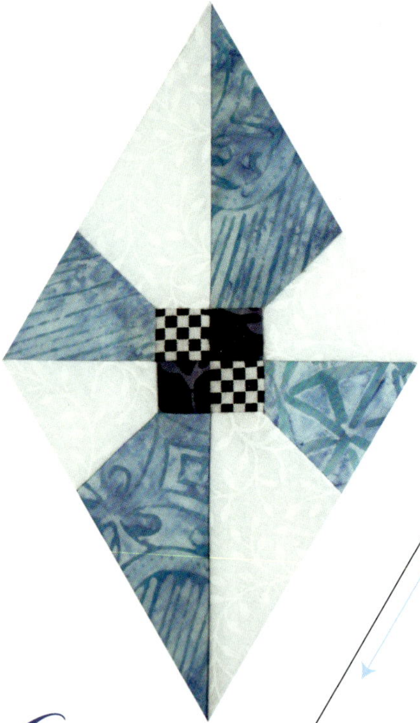

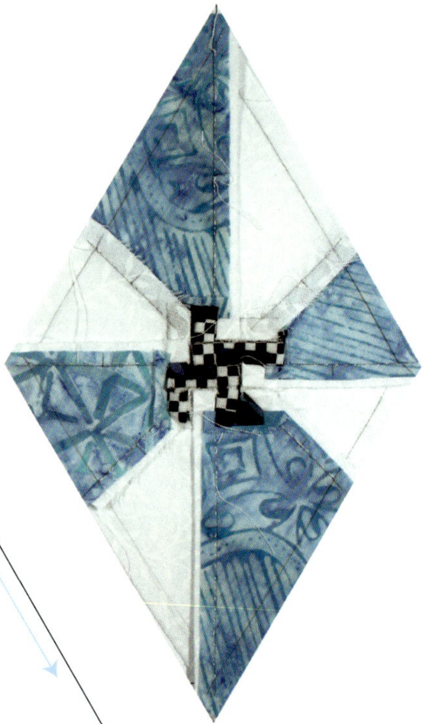

6

She was come to be happy, and she felt happy already.

*(NA Ch 2) They arrived at Bath. Catherine was all eager delight;—her eyes were
here, there, everywhere, as they approached its fine and striking environs,
and afterwards drove through those streets which conducted them to the hotel.*

Press one intersection at a
time with the seam allowances
radiating around the intersection
in one direction (clockwise or
counterclockwise) and finger the

seam allowances open to lie flat.
Freezer paper templates produce
the mirror image. Compare the
placement of the fabrics on the back
and front of the turquoise diamond.

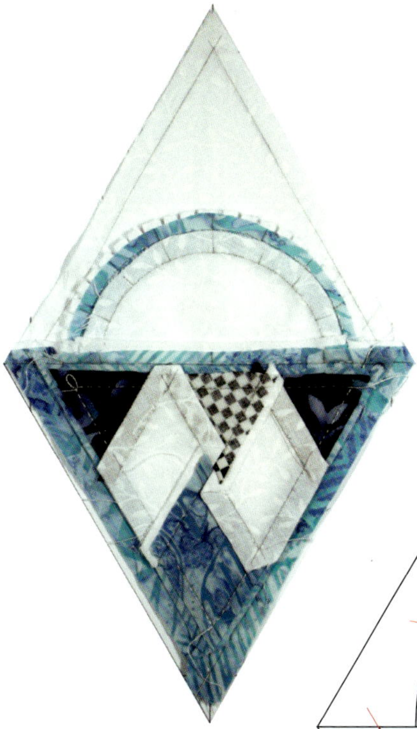

A single woman, of good fortune, is always respectable.

(E Ch 10) *"But still, you will be an old maid! and that's so dreadful!"*
Harriet wonders why Emma is not interested in marriage.

You may choose to appliqué the basket handle but these curves are easy to piece by hand and they press well.

Try sewing one curve with the unclipped side up and the other curve with the clipped side up and decide which is easier for you.

Linda Franz

17

8

It was now her darling object.

(S&S Ch 50) Mrs. Dashwood was acting on motives of policy as well as pleasure
in the frequency of her visits at Delaford; for her wish of bringing
Marianne and Colonel Brandon together...was now her darling object.

The three center wedges can be
joined with one thread, turning at
the point, for continuous stitching,
as on page 122.

When you start pinning the curve,
notice that the top patch lines up
over the three center wedges only.

Quilted Diamonds 2

9

There should be moderation in everything.

(MP Ch 32) Sir Thomas visits Fanny in the East Room and learns that she is never allowed the comfort of a fire.
Your aunt Norris has always been an advocate, and very judiciously, for young people's being brought up without unnecessary indulgences; but there should be moderation in everything.

This design allows for continuous stitching. Stitch down one side of the center diamonds, joining the half diamonds as you go...

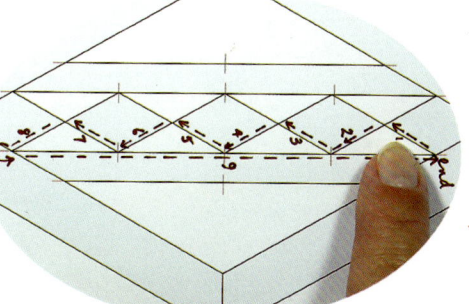

...and then turn another corner to add the narrow strip to the other side of the half diamonds, lining up each match, one at a time.

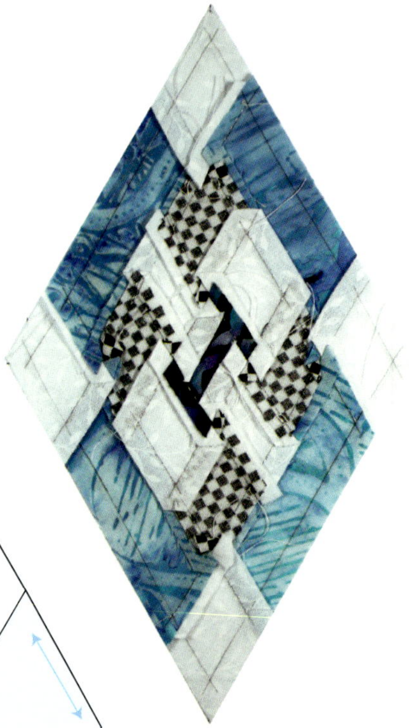

10

Nothing could be pleasanter.

(E Ch 13) This is quite the season indeed for friendly meetings.
At Christmas everybody invites their friends about them,
and people think little of even the worst weather.

With continuous stitching, the nine-patch can be sewn in a herringbone style with only four threads. Use the crosshairs for perfect matches!

If continuous stitching (page 118) is not your cup of tea, join the pieces in strips the way you would for machine piecing.

Quilted Diamonds 2

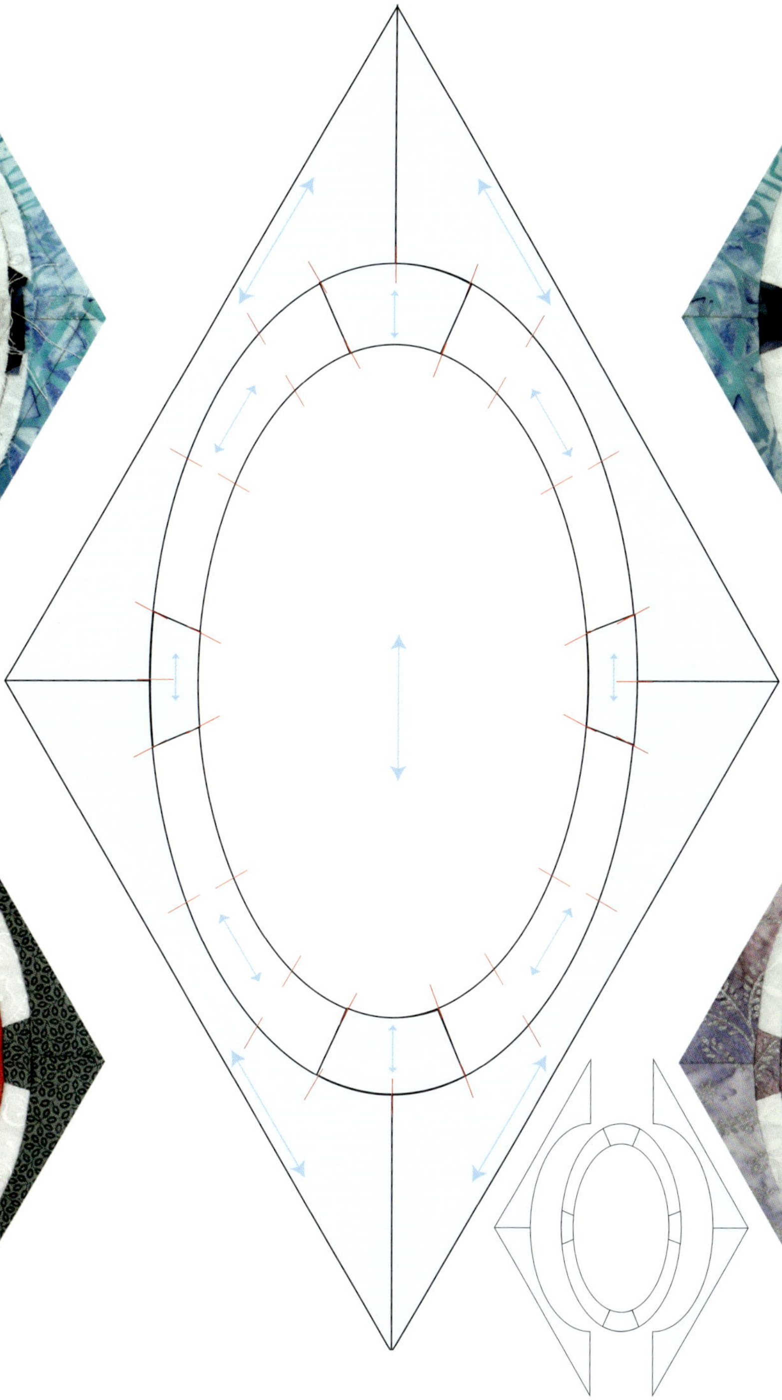

It takes a bend or two, but nothing of consequence.

(P Ch 21) Gossip travels quickly in Bath. *Mr. Elliot talks unreservedly
to Colonel Wallis of his views on* Anne—which Colonel Wallis tells *his very pretty silly wife,
who repeats it all to Nurse Rooke, who very naturally tells Anne's friend,* Mrs. Smith.

You may find these gentle curves even easier to stitch if you cut the seam allowance slightly narrower than ¼ inch and clip every 1/8 inch where the curve is tight.

Add more matching marks between the ones shown. You can decide to ignore them later if you don't need them.

Linda Franz

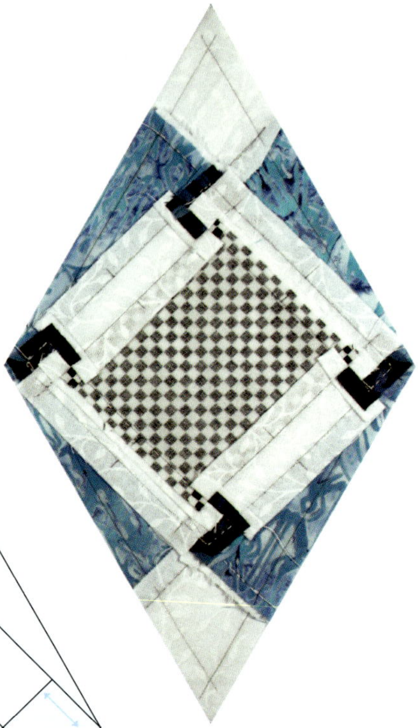

12

It was really a very handsome thought.

(P&P Ch 18) Mr. Collins introduced himself to Mr. Darcy at a ball, and
"He answered me with the utmost civility...It was really a very handsome thought.
Upon the whole, I am much pleased with him." Elizabeth doubts Mr. Darcy would return the compliment.

You can use a sewing sequence similar to what you would use by machine, or use continuous stitching, sometimes finishing two seams with one thread...

...and sometimes four.

Doesn't this cat look contented with the salmon hand dye? *Upon the whole, I am much pleased with him.*

Quilted Diamonds 2

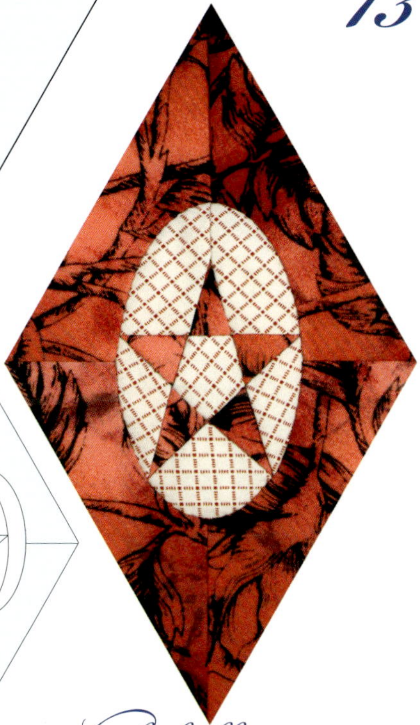

The nights are moonlight, and we shall do delightfully.

(NA Ch 11) Isabella wants to see Blaize Castle. "We shall have a most heavenly drive...
Oh! I am in such ecstasies at the thoughts of a little country air and quiet!"

Five-pointed stars have been favorites of mine ever since I learned to draw them as a little girl, with a continuous line. Now I like to stitch a continuous line.

I have shown another common sewing sequence above. *We shall do delightfully* making diamonds and ovals with curves and stars.

Linda Franz

14

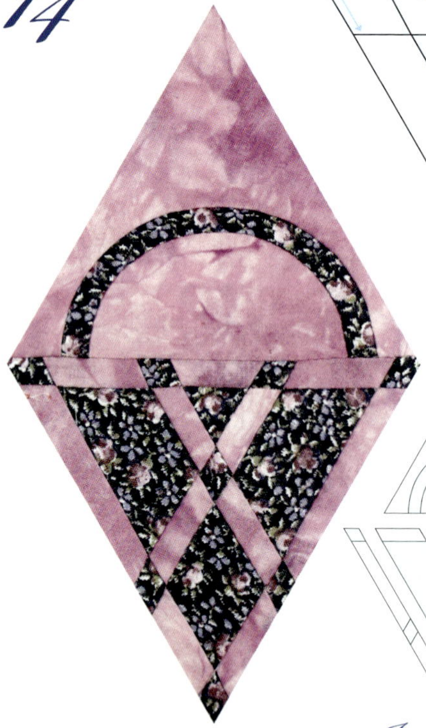

I never saw anything so charming!

(S&S Ch 19) Mrs. Palmer...was hardly seated before her admiration of the parlour and everything in it burst forth. "Well! what a delightful room this is! I never saw anything so charming!"

This basket presses well. The seams in the basket handle press toward the top of the diamond, covering the clipped seam allowances.

If you start at the bottom, you will find you can make almost all of the seams radiate around the intersections and that reduces the bulk and makes the quilting easier.

Quilted Diamonds 2

Every pane was so large, so clear, so light!

(NA Ch 20) *To an imagination which had hoped for the smallest divisions, and the heaviest stonework, for painted glass, dirt and cobwebs, the difference was very distressing.*

In the black and gold diamond I ignored the suggested straight grain when I "fussy cut" the flower for the center.

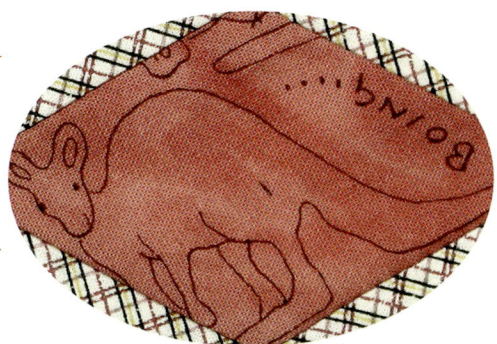

This diamond can be pressed so every seam radiates around an intersection, making the diamond look its best and making the quilting easier.

Linda Franz

16

From a variety of causes, she was happy.

(MP Ch 28) Fanny is ready for her first ball. *She had nothing more to wish for. She had hardly ever been in a state so nearly approaching high spirits in her life.*

This design allows continuous stitching, if you like to work that way. Press one intersection at a time with the seam allowances fanned around the intersections.

I ignored the suggested grain line on the center piece to "fussy cut" the tea cups. When there is bias on the outside edges, be especially careful not to stretch it out of shape!

It must be an amusing study.

(P&P Ch 9) Mr. Bingley and Elizabeth are studiers of character.
"Yes; but intricate characters are the most amusing. They have at least that advantage."

All of the star points can be stitched
continuously and then added to the
center oval. You may find it easier if
the seam allowances on the curves
are slightly less than ¼ inch wide.

The beige fabric with the small circle
design is thick compared to the
others and that made the diamond
more difficult to stitch.

Linda Franz

18

There were shady lanes wherever they wanted to go.

(MP Ch 7) A young party is always provided with a shady lane.
Four fine mornings successively were spent in this manner, in showing
the Crawfords the country, and doing the honors of its finest spots.

This one looks great in two, three or four fabrics. The curves are gentle and easy for a beginner. See page 123 and the DVD lesson for tips for stitching curves.

Remember to clip the concave seam allowance between the matches, about every 1/3 inch on these gentle curves.

Quilted Diamonds 2

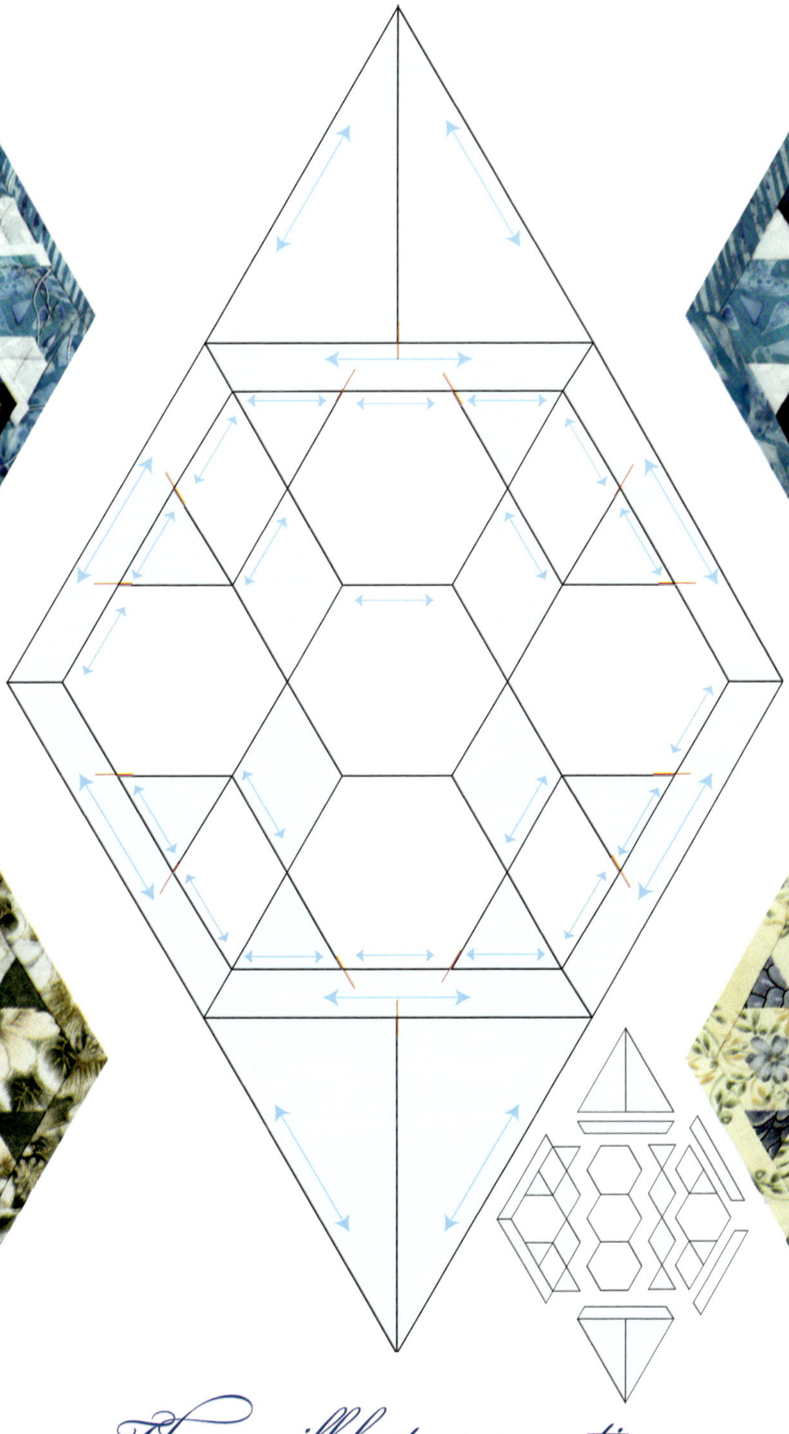

Those will last us some time.

(NA Ch 6) "Castle of Wolfenbach, Clermont, Mysterious Warnings, Necromancer of the Black Forest, Midnight Bell, Orphan of the Rhine, and Horrid Mysteries. Those will last us some time." Catherine and Isabella are reading novels together.

Notice how the intersections press perfectly in a radiating manner so this diamond lies flat. This design looks very different in 2, 3 or 4 fabrics.

Thirty-one pieces *will last us some time* but maybe not as long as you think! I took 5 stitches per short seam, turning at the end of seams when I could, to stitch continuously.

Linda Franz

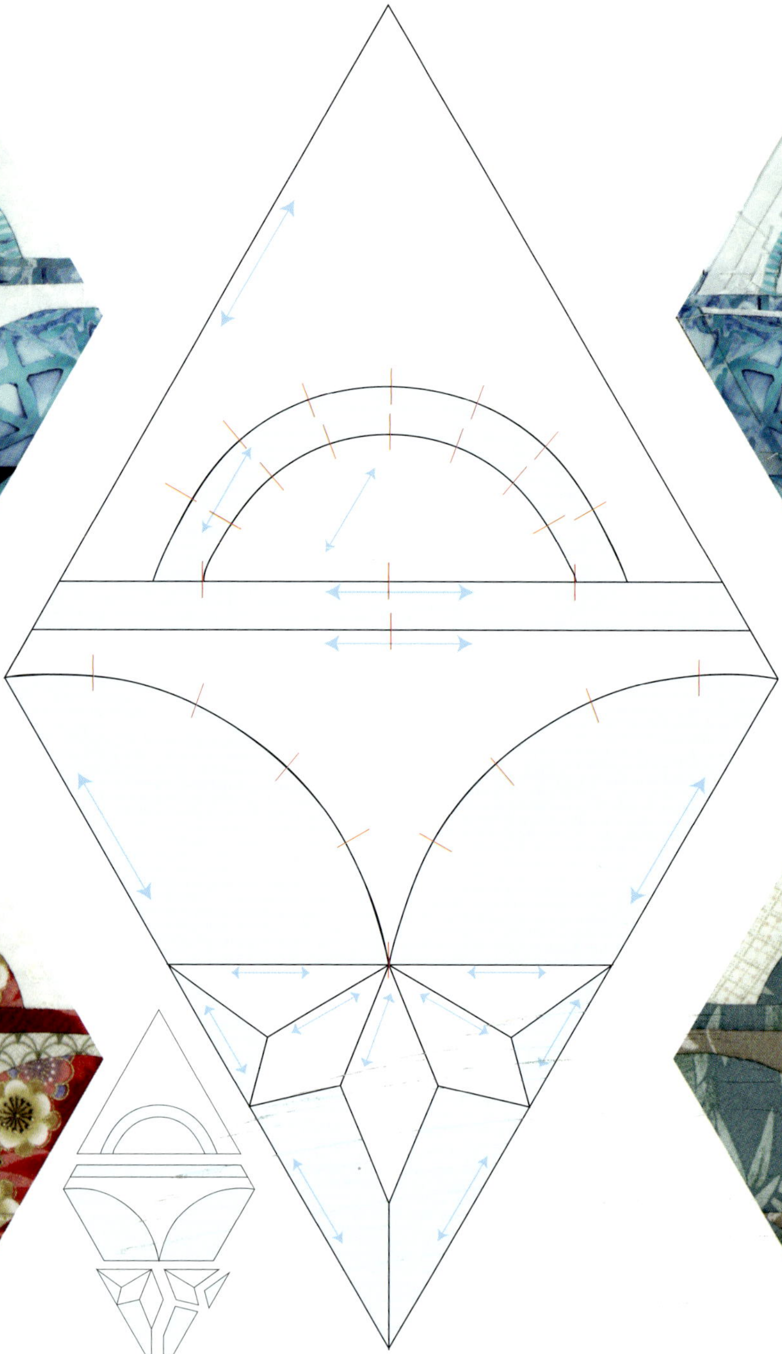

20

Living to be fashionable, happy, and merry.

(P Ch 5) *Henrietta and Louisa, young ladies of nineteen and twenty...were now, like thousands of other young ladies, living to be fashionable, happy, and merry. Their dress had every advantage, their faces were rather pretty, their spirits extremely good, their manners unembarrassed and pleasant;*

This elegant design has it all—curves, insets and many seams converging. Use crosshairs and matches and see pages 122-123.

The curves are gentle and the whole diamond presses well. Monkey thinks you can make a good impression with this one.

21

Handsome, elegant, highly accomplished, and perfectly amiable.

(E Ch 22) A week had not passed since Miss Hawkins's name was first mentioned in Highbury, before she was, by some means or other, discovered to have every recommendation of person and mind.

This simple design creates a nice opportunity for "fussy cutting" and you can ignore the suggested grain on the center piece if you like.

Monkey thinks the frog is more *handsome, elegant, highly accomplished, and perfectly amiable* than Miss Hawkins, the future wife of Mr. Elton.

Linda Franz

22

I never spent a pleasanter morning in my life.

(S&S Ch 13) Marianne and Willoughby *had gone to Allenham, and spent a considerable time there in walking about the garden and going all over the house.*

The pale blue diamond is a little bit disappointing to me because there is not enough contrast in the three fabrics. I made up for it in the black and white one!

Using matches and crosshairs makes precision a pleasure and the mitered border allows straight grain on all the outside edges.

23

So we must all be as merry as we can.

(P Ch 6) Mr and Mrs Musgrove need cheering up, and
all the relief which cheerful companions could give.

When many seams converge, you might like to "circle the intersection" as shown on page 123 and on the DVD.

On curves, load only one or two stitches at a time and backstitch about every ½ inch, as usual.

24

If not quite handsome, was very near it.

(NA Ch 3) His name was Tilney. He seemed to be about four or five and twenty, was rather tall, had a pleasing countenance, a very intelligent and lively eye, and, if not quite handsome, was very near it.

I got into a nice rhythm with five stitches per seam, backstitching at the beginning and the end.

I used a white marker on the plaid. It disappears when ironed. Don't forget to mark the matches too!

25

Elegance, sweetness, beauty.

(P Ch 14) Oh! there was no end of Miss Elliot's charms.

Curves, many seams converging and inset seams—a nightmare for machine piecers! One of the curved seams needs to be pressed to bend back on itself.

My pink diamond went through the wash with some table napkins, by accident, after a dinner with friends when I was showing off my newborn diamonds—and it survived!

26

Everything delightful to her.

*(S&S Ch 45) Mrs. Dashwood had an active fancy, which fashioned
everything delightful to her, as it chose.*

My friend, Mary Althaus, hand
pieced the turquoise diamond for me
with her tiny stitches. She taught
me how to hand piece in January
1998, and I am very grateful!

There is only one other diamond in
the book that I did not stitch myself.

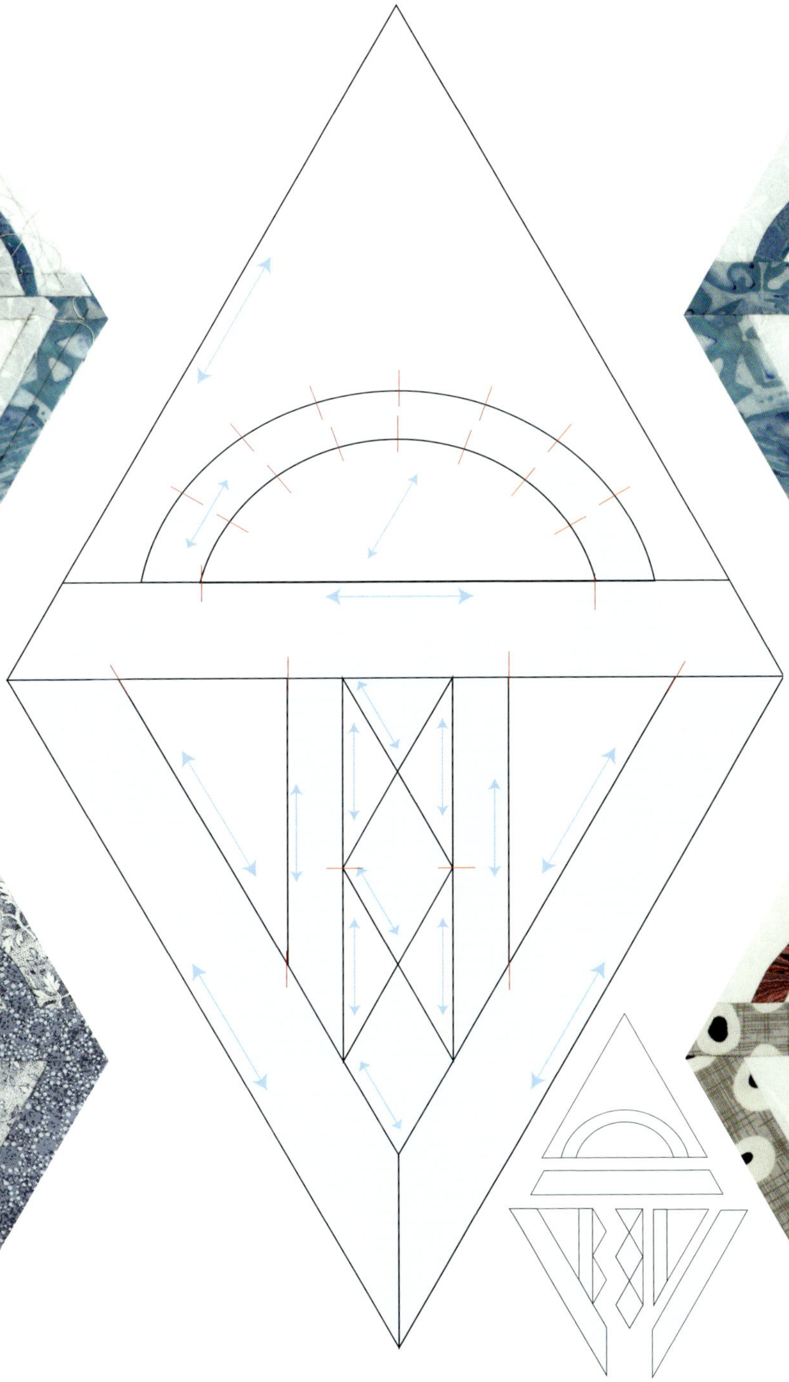

27

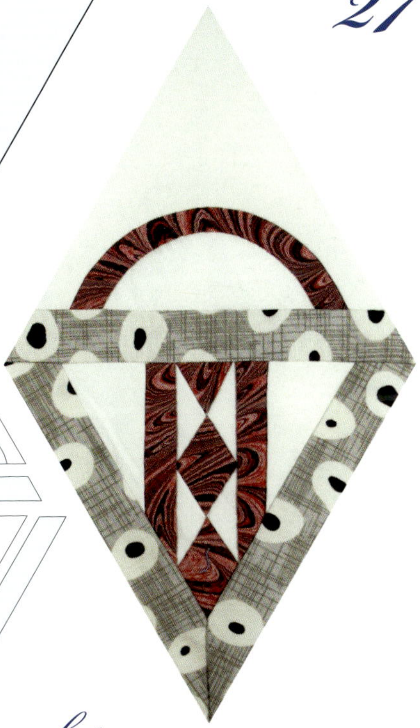

I could not help making a treasure of it.

(E Ch 40) She held the parcel towards her, and Emma read the words Most precious treasures on the top.
Her curiosity was greatly excited. Harriet has been saving mementos of Mr. Elton.

I generally avoid using ivory sateen and muslin, partly because I like the weave and weight to be similar to the other fabrics and...

...also because I prefer more interest in the background fabric. Tone-on-tones and hand dyes make great backgrounds.

28

I wanted to be doing something.

(P Ch 8) Captain Wentworth: *"It was a great object with me, at that time, to be at sea,—a very great object. I wanted to be doing something."*

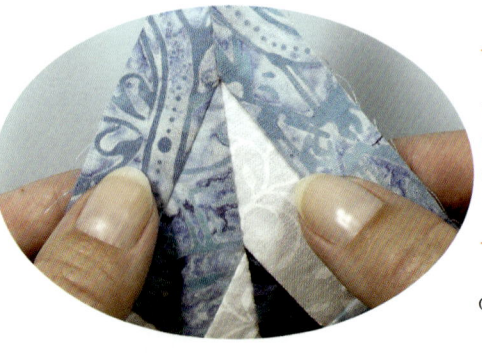

I often use white or ivory thread that matches the background fabric, but I try to use thread that matches the color of the fabric when stitching two darker fabrics together, in this case, turquoise.

Her model of the amiable and pleasing.

*(P&P Ch 27) The farewell between herself and Mr. Wickham was perfectly friendly;
on his side even more....and she parted from him convinced, that whether married or single,
he must always be her model of the amiable and pleasing.*

Sew all the triangles to the center square with one thread, turning at each corner to speed up the sewing.

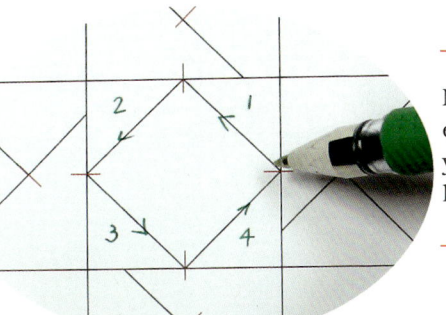

Notice how the matches help keep everything lined up perfectly when you are stitching. This diamond looks great in 2, 3 or 4 fabrics.

30

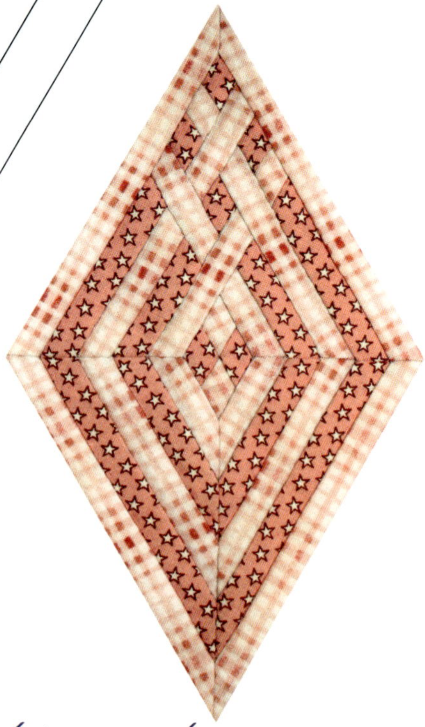

A worthy employment for a young lady's mind!

(E Ch 1) Mr. Knightley does not think Emma should be matchmaking.
"A straightforward, openhearted man, like Weston, and a rational unaffected woman,
like Miss Taylor, may be safely left to manage their own concerns."

I have stitched this diamond three times and every time I found a different sewing sequence. The center pieces near the top require an odd approach, with insets and

"jagged" rows, but the effect of the knot design is worth it for me.

I hope you will find it to be *a worthy employment* for you.

Quilted Diamonds 2

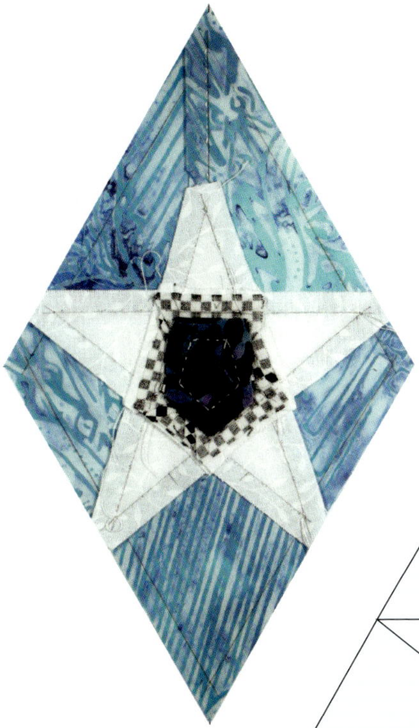

Her most exquisite enjoyment.

(S&S Ch 10) His society became gradually her most exquisite enjoyment. They read, they talked, they sang together. Marianne is falling in love with Willoughby.

First, I stitch one border on the center, then turn the corner at the crosshair to make the miter with the second border piece, then stitch that border to the center, and so on, until

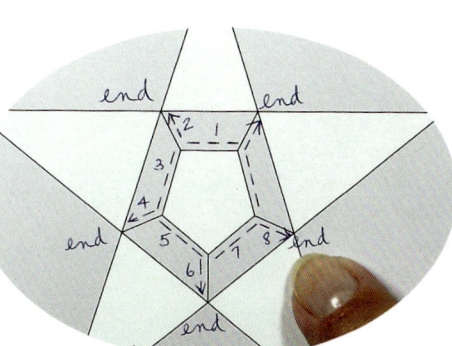

all five borders are on.

If you are having trouble threading, turn the needle around. The eye is stamped so it might be easier to thread from the other side.

32

Yes, that would be quite enough for pleasure.

(E Ch 29) There is to be a dance in Highbury. *"You and Miss Smith, and Miss Fairfax,
will be three, and the two Miss Coxes five; and for five couples there will be plenty of room."*

This diamond presses well with
many seams radiating and the
curves on the handle pressed
toward the top of the diamond.

Quite enough pleasant continuous
stitching is possible. The crosshairs
and matches are your guarantee of
precision.

33

It was, indeed, a highly prized letter.

(E Ch 2) For a few days every morning visit in Highbury included
some mention of the handsome letter Mrs. Weston had received.

The center of this diamond provides
a great opportunity for "fussy
cutting."

The matches on the long seams will
help you keep everything aligned
when you are stitching.

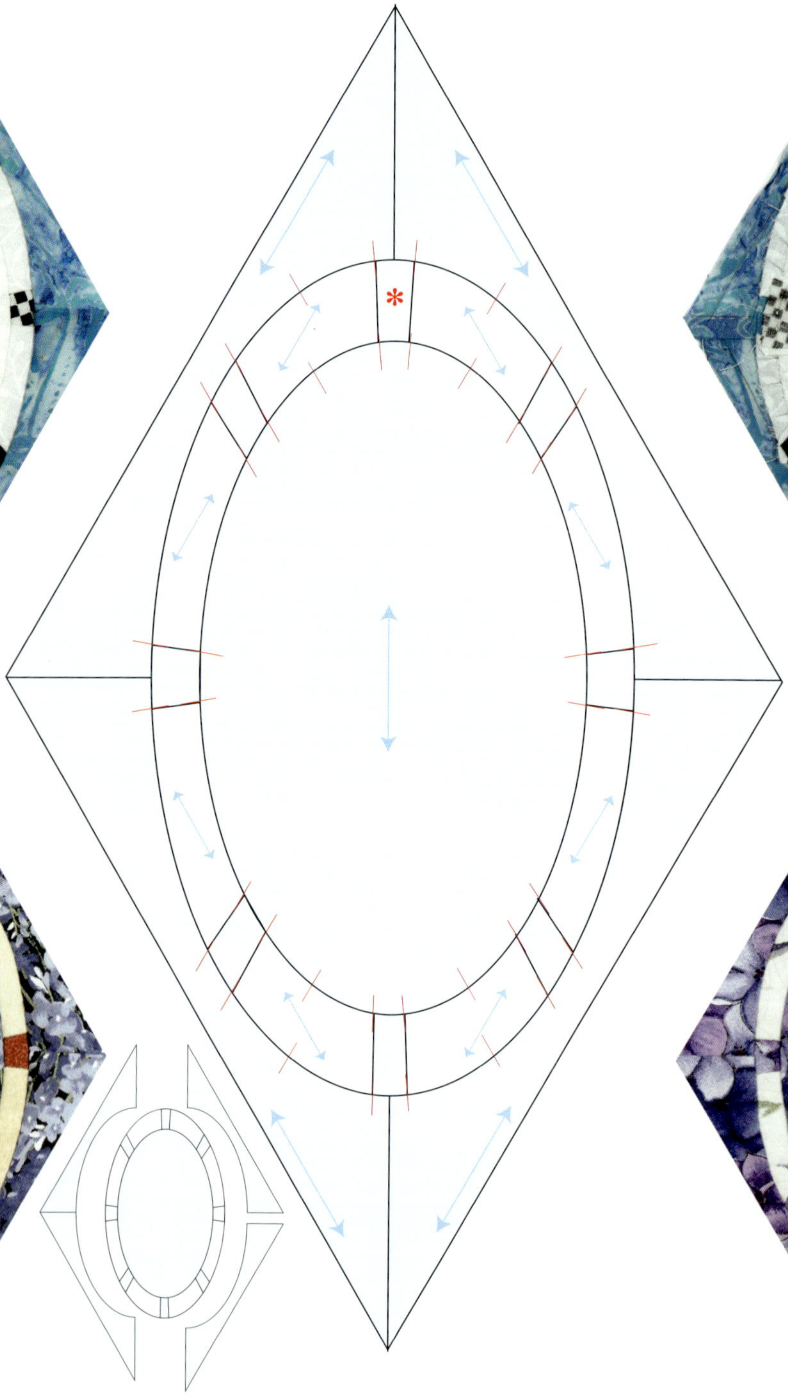

34

There was so much of friendliness.

(P Ch 9) There was so much of friendliness, and of flattery, and of everything most bewitching
in his reception there; the old were so hospitable, the young so agreeable,
that he could not but resolve to remain where he was.

A friend from Texas gave me a
wonderful fabric for this diamond. It
is okay to ignore the suggested grain
line on the center oval, as shown
here with the monkey.

You do not need to cut on straight
grain for tiny interior * pieces.
Monkey suggests using more clips
on the tightest parts of the curve
and pinning one match at a time.

Some shelves in the closets upstairs.

(P&P Ch 14) Lady Catherine *had once paid him a visit in his humble parsonage;*
where she had perfectly approved all the alterations he had been making,
and had even vouchsafed to suggest some herself,—some shelves in the closets upstairs.

Cut off long points (beyond ¼ inch)
when you are rotary cutting. You will
trim your finished diamonds anyway
and in the meantime they can catch
your thread. See page 115.

You can compare the front and back
of the turquoise diamond to see the
effect of mirror image. (Also see page
118.)

Linda Franz

36

Is not this an agreeable surprise?

(P&P Ch 39) "And we mean to treat you all," added Lydia; "but you must lend us the money,
for we have just spent ours at the shop out there."

This diamond's inset seams would
be difficult on the sewing machine
but they are easy to hand piece.

Is not this an agreeable surprise?
See page 122 and the DVD lesson
for suggestions for inset seams.

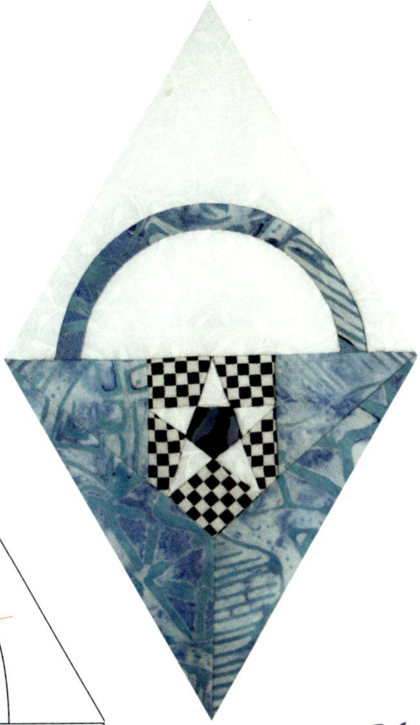

This is precisely what I wanted.

(E Ch 35) But it is an excellent thing to have Frank among us again, so near as town.
They will stay a good while when they do come, and he will be half his time with us. This is precisely what I wanted.

You may modify this diamond to get precisely what you want! "Fussy cut" a flower or other motif in your fabric and replace the eleven pieces in the star with only one.

You can simplify any diamond any time just by eliminating lines when you are tracing, or when you are cutting, or with the optional *QD2 CD* and Electric Quilt.

Linda Franz

38

The pleasantest part of the day.

(E Ch 42) Emma and her friends picked strawberries at Donwell Abbey.
They took a few turns together along the walk.—The shade was most refreshing,
and Emma found it the pleasantest part of the day.

Although I normally use ivory or white thread, I try to match the fabric color when I am stitching a

seam with two dark fabrics, as when joining the two large triangles to the hexagon. I used brown thread here.

Quilted Diamonds 2

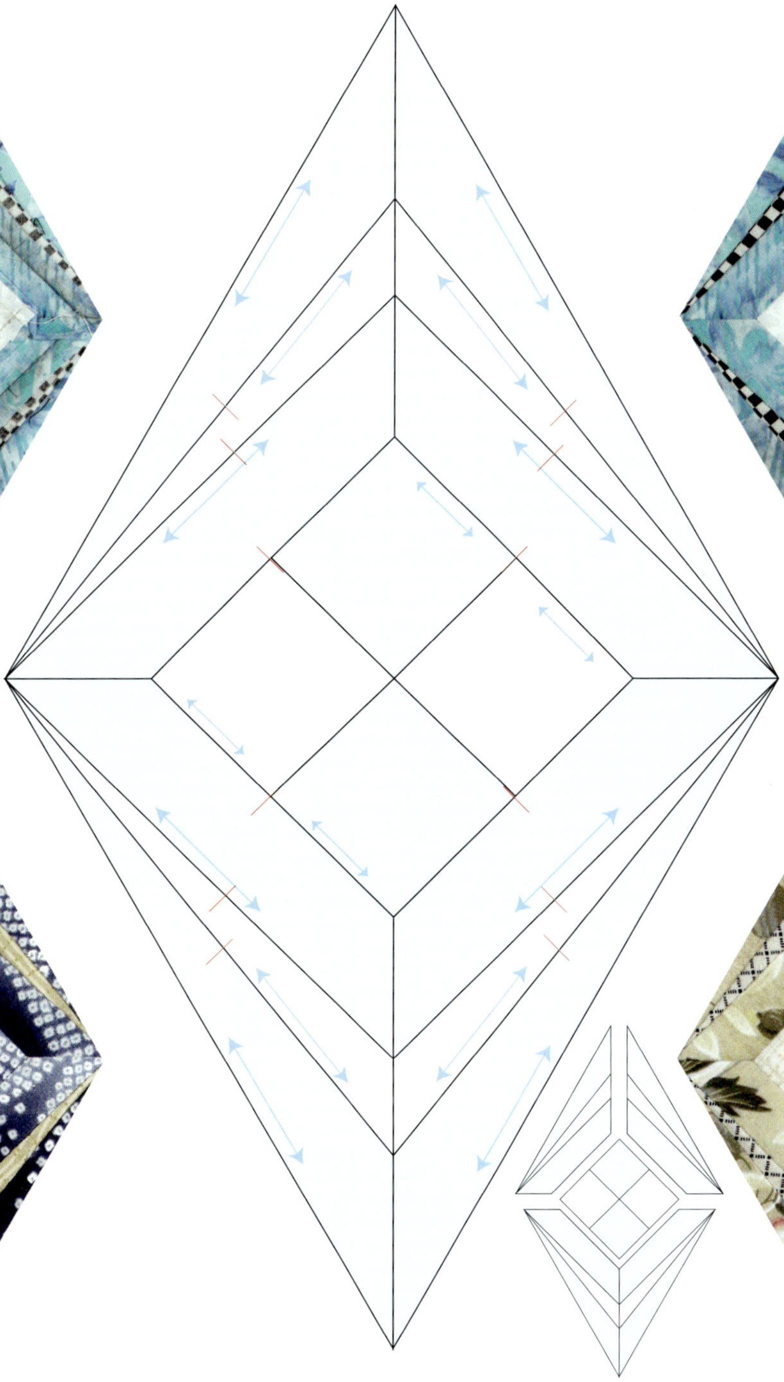

Two delightful twilight walks.

(S&S Ch 42) Marianne and Elinor pause in their journey at Cleveland, the home of the Palmers.
Two delightful twilight walks on the third and fourth evenings, in damp weather,
give Marianne a violent, dangerous cold.

On very sharp points, you may find it helpful to add a third line inside the normal crosshair, as described on page 123 and on the DVD, to make the seams line up better.

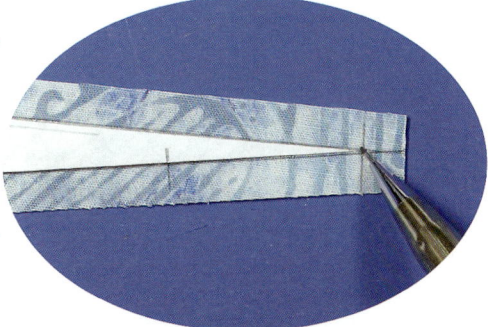

I don't always mark the third line anymore but I will compensate by pinning slightly inside the crosshair even when I have not marked the spot.

40

A mine of felicity to herself.

*(E Ch 3) The simplicity and cheerfulness of her nature, her contented and grateful spirit,
were a recommendation to everybody and a mine of felicity to herself.*

You can see the effect of mirror image by comparing the front and the back of the turquoise diamond. The fabrics on the back are on the opposite side on the front.

You might want to take this into account when you make your templates. (Also see page 118 and the DVD.) Mark more matches than those on the pattern if you like.

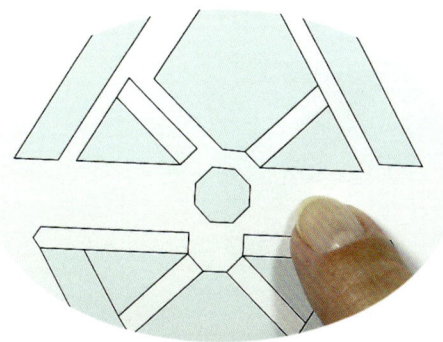

A fresh source of happiness.

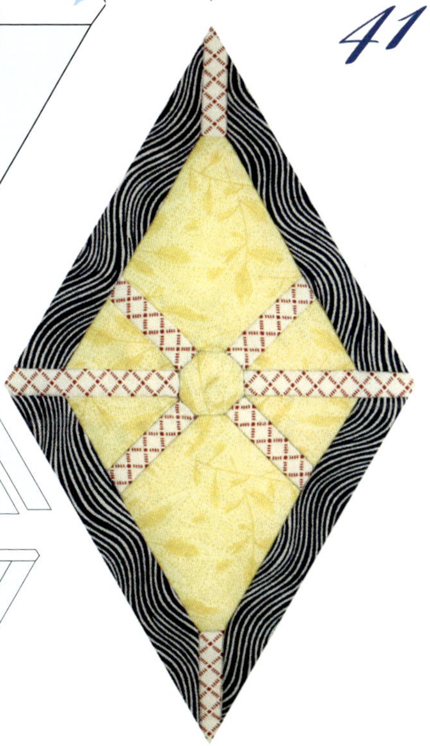

*(P&P Ch 55) Elizabeth's congratulations were given with a sincerity, a warmth, a delight,
which words could but poorly express. Every sentence of kindness was a fresh source of happiness to Jane.*

You might want to pay attention to this little sewing sequence diagram. The sequence is a bit odd, but it is not difficult.

Wet thread swells and is harder to

insert through the eye of the needle. Try flattening the thread between your fingers and licking the eye of the needle instead. The moisture is supposed to attract the thread.

42

This of course made everybody laugh.

(S&S Ch 12) Margaret unwittingly reveals too much to Mrs. Jennings about Elinor's favorite young man. *His name begins with an F.*

Very small interior * pieces like these do not need to be on straight grain, and don't worry, they look a little bigger with the seam allowance. You can do it!

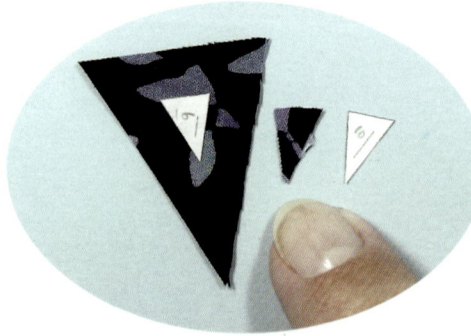

This design looks great in two, three or four fabrics, but the quality makes a huge difference. Coarse, loosely woven fabrics are not suitable! Thinner is better!

Quilted Diamonds 2

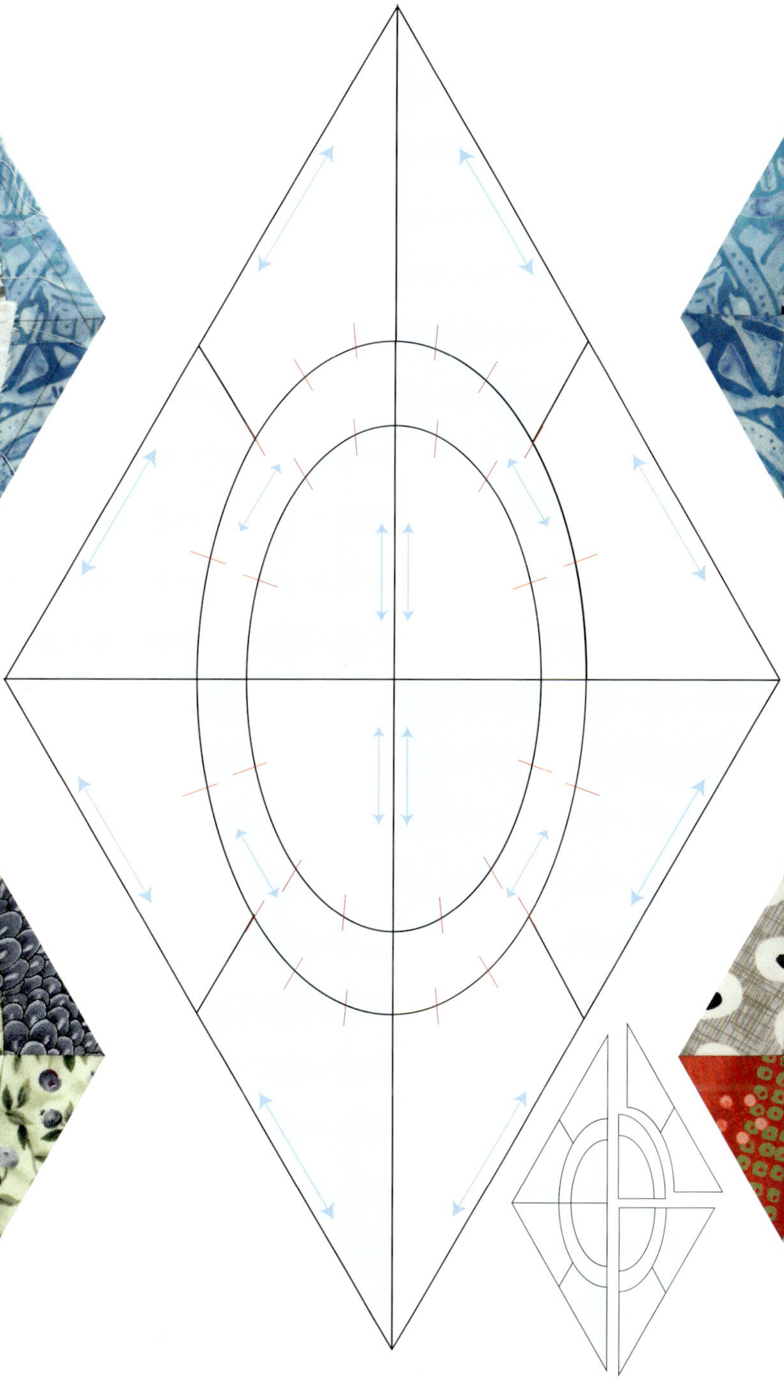

43

The object of her happiest thoughts.

(P&P Ch 42) Elizabeth's *tour to the Lakes was now the object of her happiest thoughts;*
it was her best consolation. She set her heart on it.

This diamond presses neatly with the unclipped seam allowances pressed over the clipped ones.

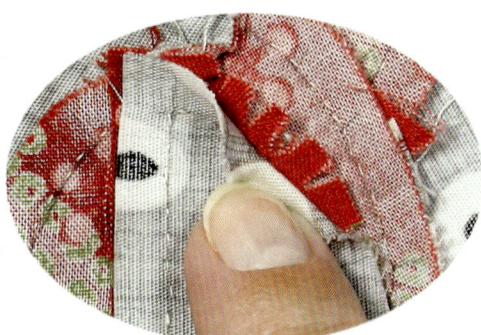

Don't worry about pressing to the dark. You can trim each dark seam allowance by a scant 1/8 inch when the diamond is finished to eliminate "shadowing" and reduce the bulk.

44

Little zigzags of embarrassment.

(E Ch 15) Emma and Mr. Elton have a tête-à-tête drive. *If there had not been so much anger, there would have been desperate awkwardness; but their straightforward emotions left no room for the little zigzags of embarrassment.*

Notice how freezer paper templates produce the mirror image. The black and white checked triangle is on one side on the front and on the other side on the back.

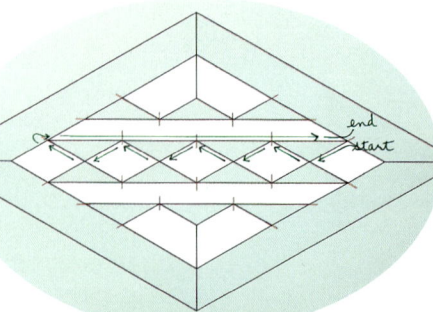

Zigzags like this create an opportunity for continuous stitching, as on page 122, and the matching marks and crosshairs guarantee precision.

Quilted Diamonds 2

Perfectly interesting in the eyes of all the ladies.

(P Ch 11) *The sympathy and goodwill excited towards
Captain Benwick was very great.*

Blue and gold for friendship!
Computers make it possible for
quilters to make new friends
without leaving home.

There are many quilters online who
enjoy hand piecing diamonds. You
can link to some of their web sites
from www.lindafranz.com.

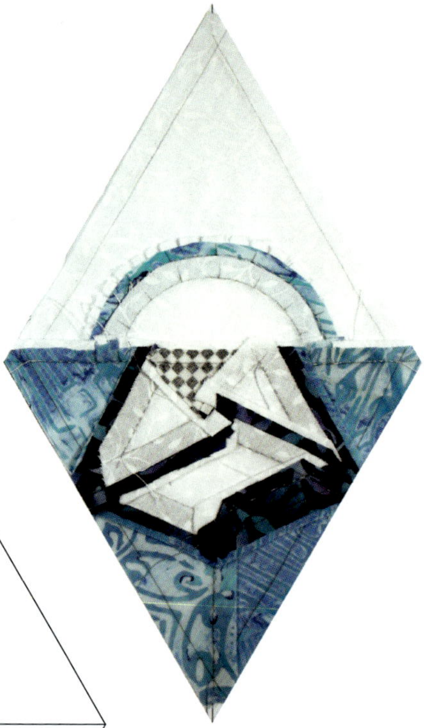

46

Necessary to amuse their morning hours.

(P&P Ch 7) A walk to Meryton was necessary to amuse their morning hours and furnish conversation for the evening.

Notice that the center diamond * should be joined to the strips on the bottom before the strips on the top edges.

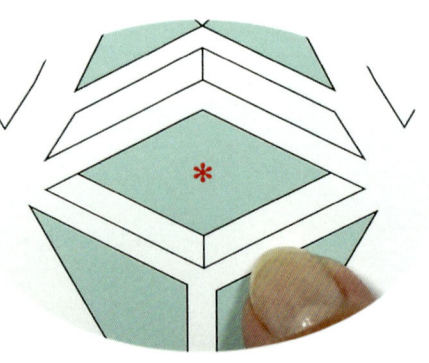

Using this sewing sequence diagram helps make this diamond go together easily.

47

Scenes had passed in Uppercross, which made it precious.

(P Ch 13) She could not quit the mansion house,
or look an adieu to the cottage...without a saddened heart.

The cross design in this diamond looks completely different in two, three or four fabrics.

Although I normally use a neutral light-colored thread, I switched to red when stitching the seams with red fabric on both sides.

48

They entered into it with pleasure.

(P Ch 10) Their time and strength, and spirits, were, therefore, exactly ready for this walk, and they entered into it with pleasure.

Slow down on curves, just taking 1 or 2 stitches at a time and backstitching every ½ inch or so.

Mark more matches on the tightest

part of the curves, if you like. Trim dark seam allowances by a scant 1/8 inch, leaving a generous 1/8 inch, when the diamond is finished.

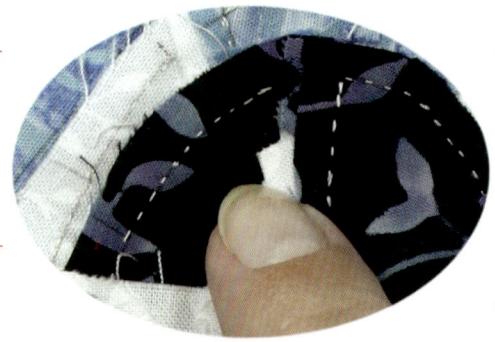

Sensible, good humored, lively.

(P&P Ch 4) "He is just what a young man ought to be," said she, "sensible, good humored, lively; and I never saw such happy manners!—so much ease, with such perfect good breeding!"

The "extra" vertical seams allow you to have straight grain on the outside edges, but you may eliminate them, if you like.

This diamond presses well, with the seam allowances radiating clockwise and counterclockwise around the intersections.

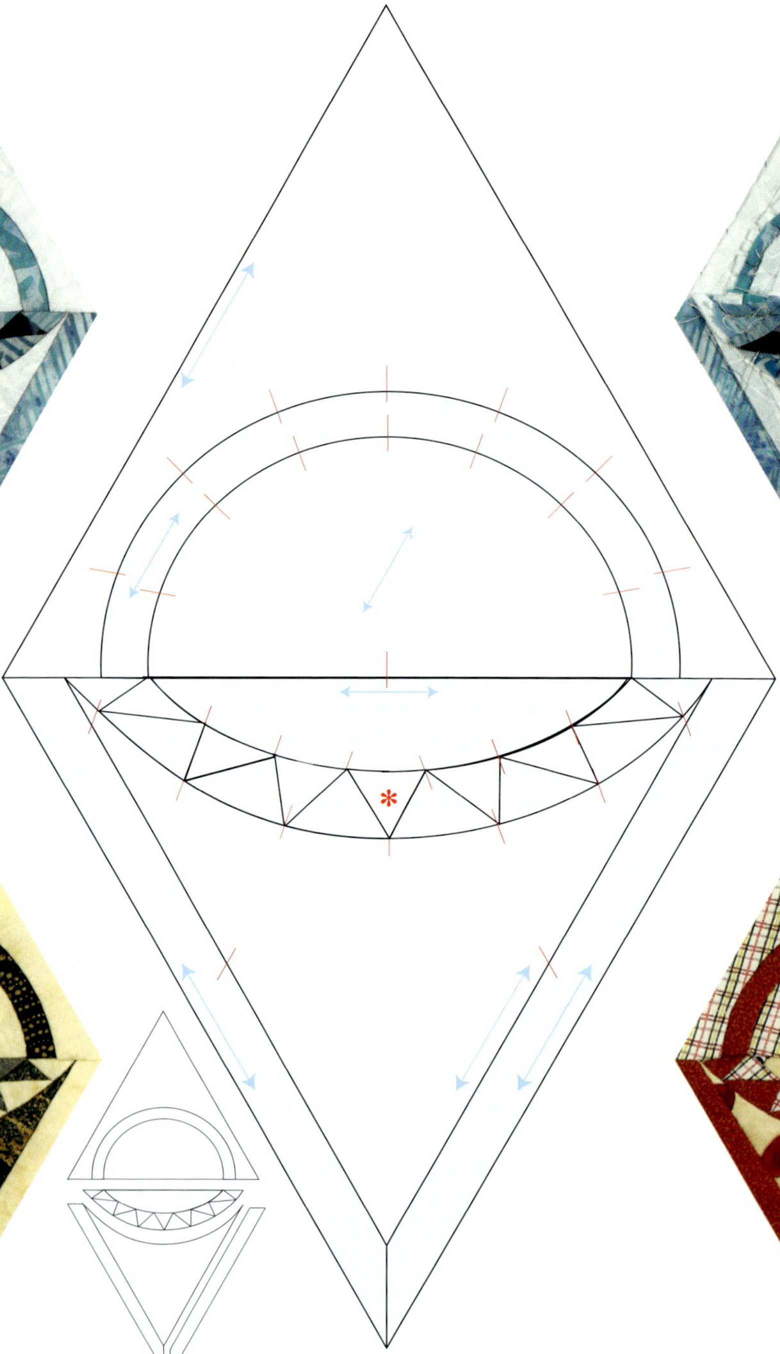

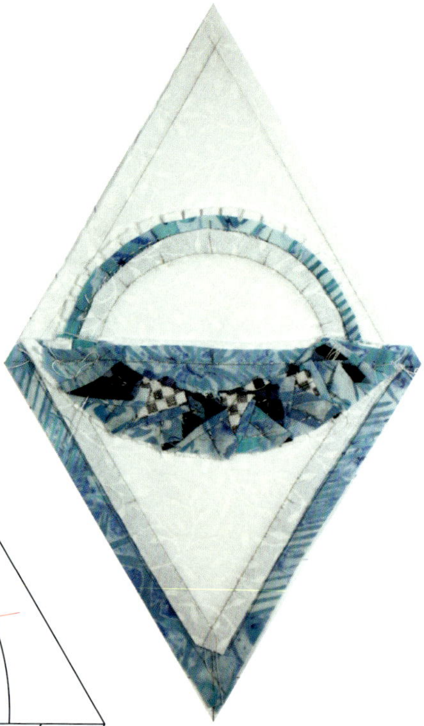

50

In high spirits and good humor, eager to be happy.

(S&S Ch 13) *Their intended excursion to Whitwell turned out very different from what Elinor had expected.*
She was prepared to be wet through, fatigued, and frightened;
but the event was still more unfortunate, for they did not go at all.

The curved strip of triangles * can
be sewn with one thread, turning at
the end of every seam, as described
on page 122 and on the DVD.

You may decide to simplify this
diamond, as I did with diamond
63, by replacing the row of
triangles with one piece.

Quilted Diamonds 2

There was novelty in the scheme.

(P&P Ch 27) March was to take Elizabeth to Hunsford...and she gradually learned
to consider it herself with greater pleasure as well as greater certainty.

You can turn these little, short seams into longer seams by continuous stitching.

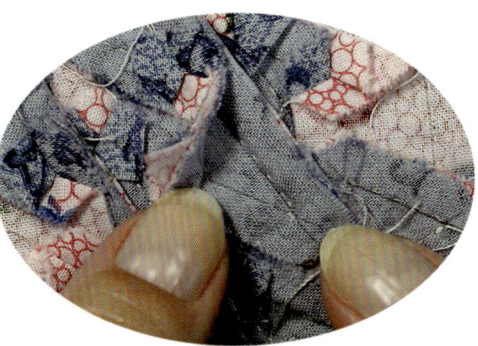

Many of these seams can be finished with one needle-load of five stitches—or even fewer.

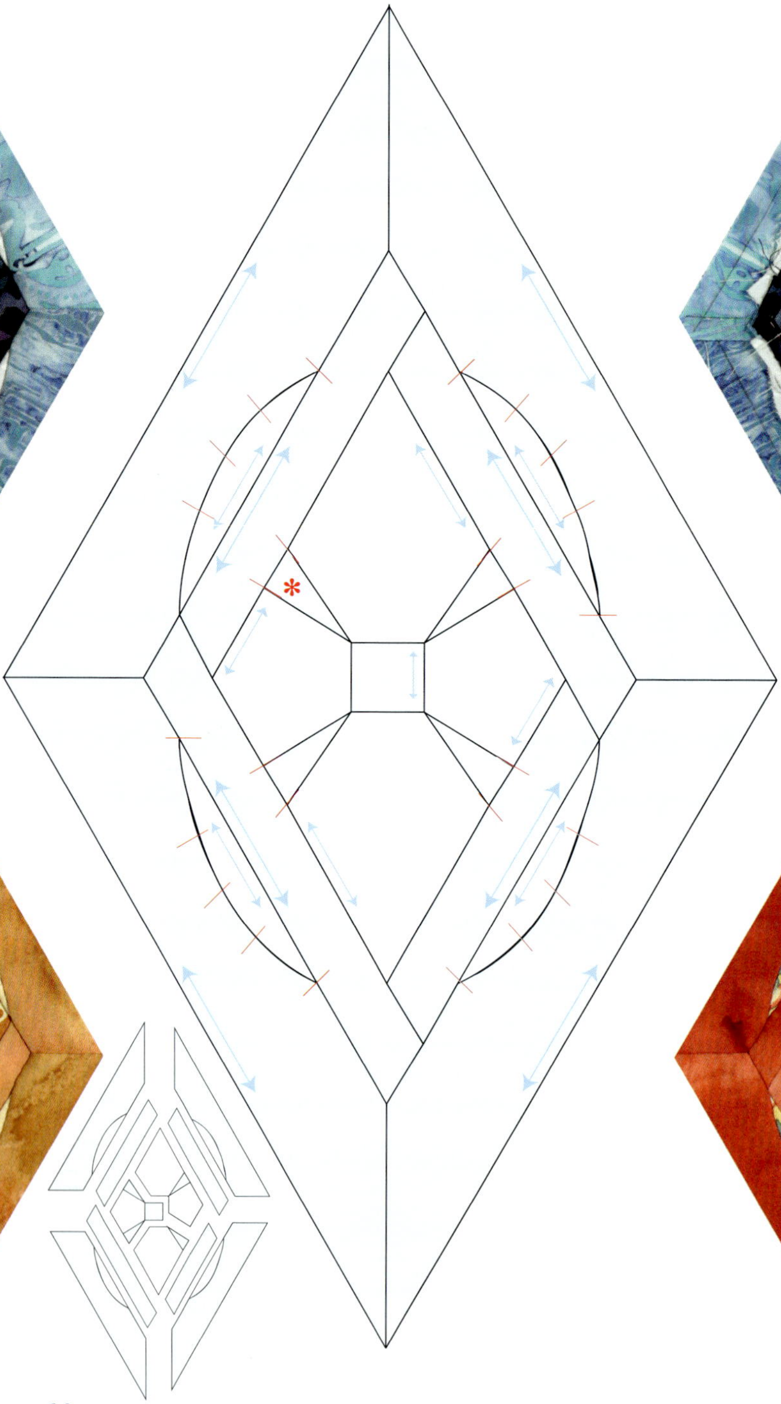

52

*

Little affairs, arrangements, perplexities and pleasures.

*(E Ch 14) To her, it was real enjoyment to be with the Westons...to whom she related
...the little affairs, arrangements, perplexities and pleasures of her father and herself.*

Marking matches will help with
the curves and the alignment of
other seams. I pin just one match
at a time. Otherwise the thread can
catch on extra pins.

Tiny interior * pieces do not need
to be cut on straight grain and that
speeds up the preparation.

Quilted Diamonds 2

He wore a blue coat and rode a black horse.

(P&P Ch 3) In a few days Mr. Bingley returned Mr. Bennet's visit,
and sat about ten minutes with him in his library.

There are 41 pieces in this diamond
but it does not take long to cut out,
as shown on page 114 and the DVD.

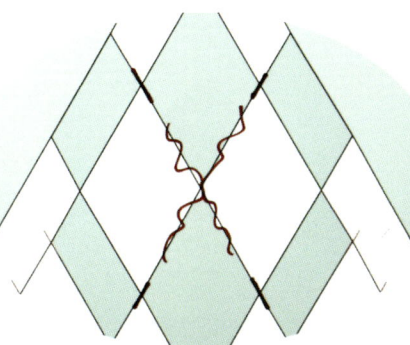

I also made the simplified version
in red and brown, with 28 pieces.
Whenever you simplify a design,
consider adding matches where you
eliminate seam lines.

Linda Franz

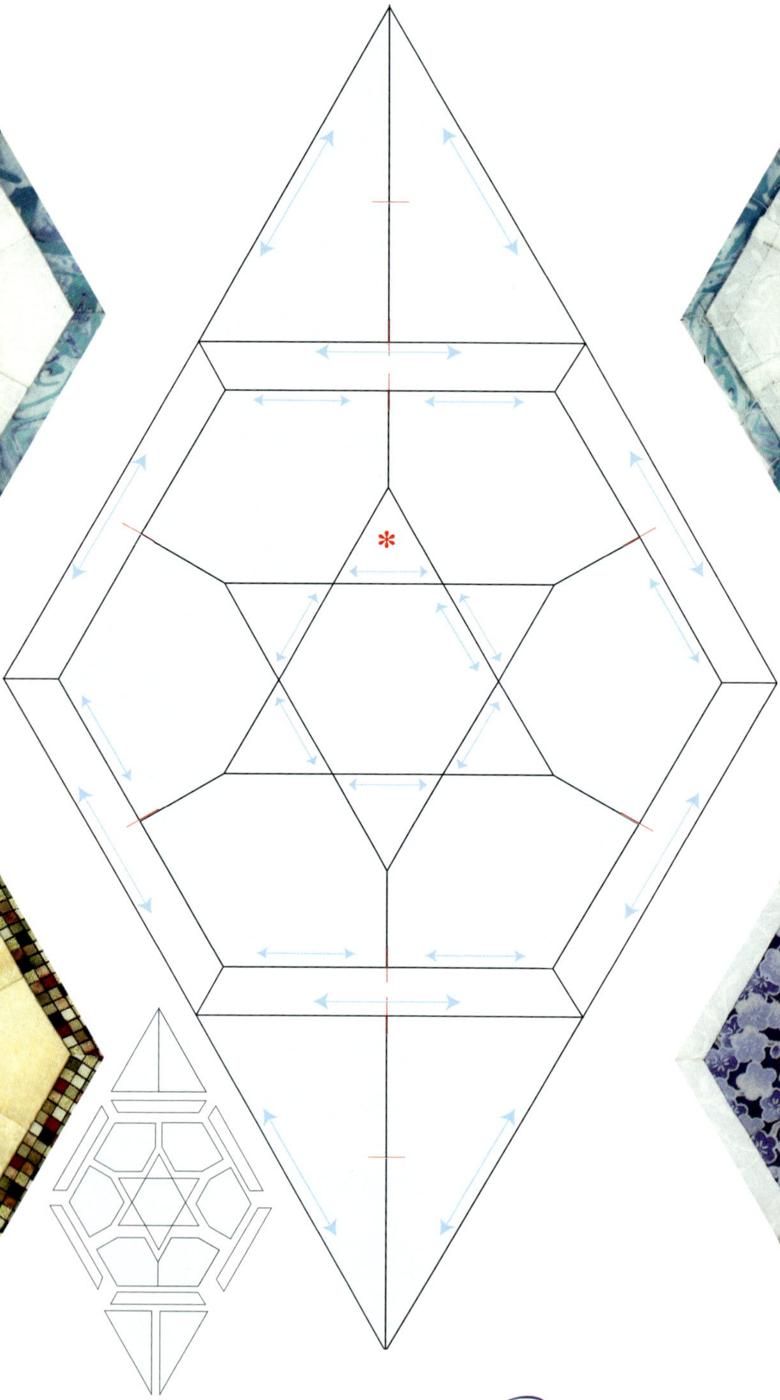

54

The influence of friendship and affection.

(P&P Ch 10) Elizabeth and Mr. Darcy discuss Mr. Bingley's character. But in general and ordinary cases between friend and friend, where one of them is desired by the other to change a resolution of no very great moment, should you think ill of that person for complying with the desire, without waiting to be argued into it?

Don't worry about cutting tiny pieces like * on grain or about pressing to the dark. You will be able to trim the dark seam allowances by 1/8 inch

(*only* the dark ones) to avoid having the dark seam allowances show through on the front, as shown on page 124 and in the DVD lesson.

Quilted Diamonds 2

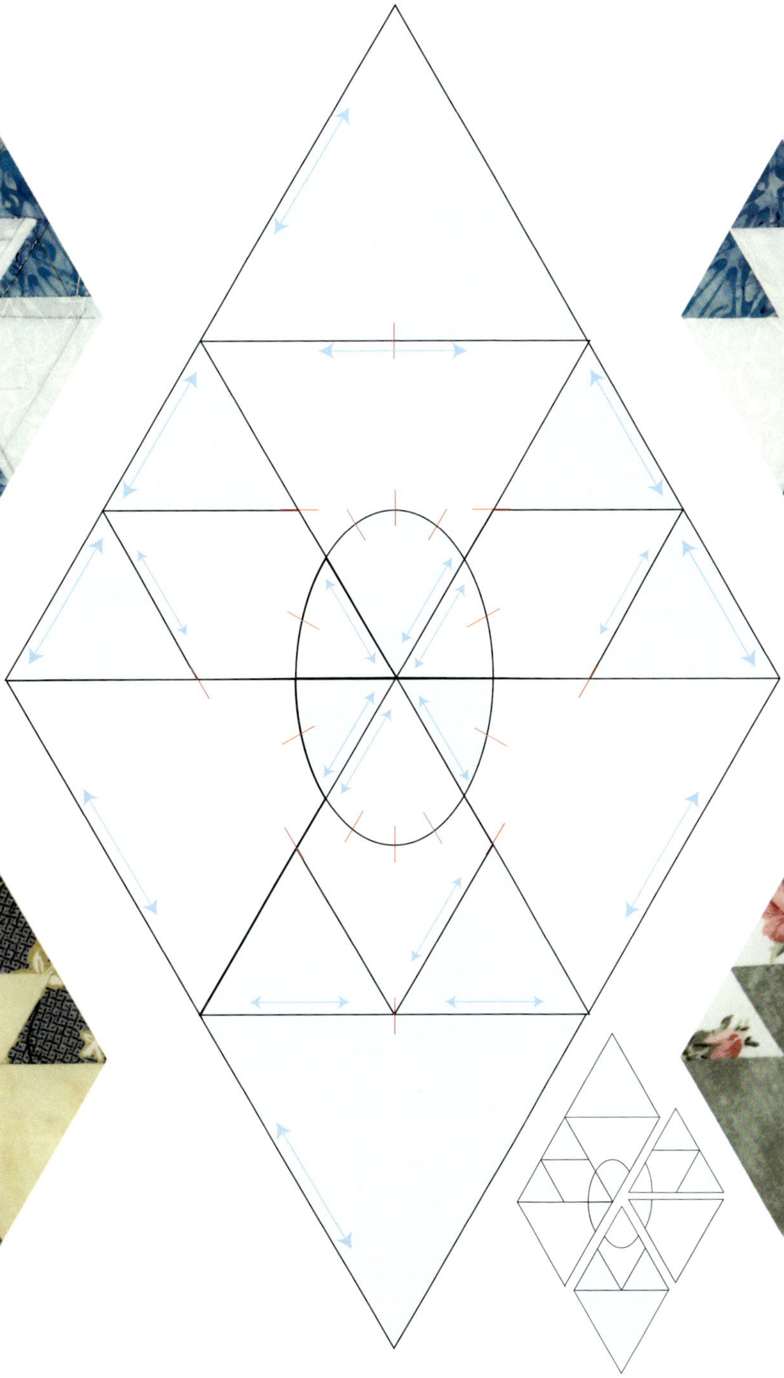

How peculiarly unlucky poor Mr. Elton was.

(E Ch 32) How peculiarly unlucky poor Mr. Elton was in being in the same room at once with
the woman he had just married, the woman he had wanted to marry, and
the woman whom he had been expected to marry.

When joining two halves of a
diamond like this, you might like
to "circle the intersection" in the
middle, as demonstrated in the DVD
lesson. Also see page 123.

It is a good idea to press all of the
seams in one direction around the
center—in a radiating manner. Test
both directions. Sometimes one
direction looks better than the other.

Linda Franz

56

Less of splendor, and more real elegance.

(P&P Ch 43) The rooms were lofty and handsome, and their furniture suitable to the fortune of their proprietor; but Elizabeth saw, with admiration of his taste, that it was neither gaudy nor uselessly fine; with less of splendor, and more real elegance, than the furniture of Rosings.

Crosshairs and matches are your guarantee of precision and this diamond will look its best with the seam allowances pressed in a radiating manner, when possible.

Be careful with the bias on the outside edges of this diamond! Pressing with steam can permanently distort the fabric.

Quilted Diamonds 2

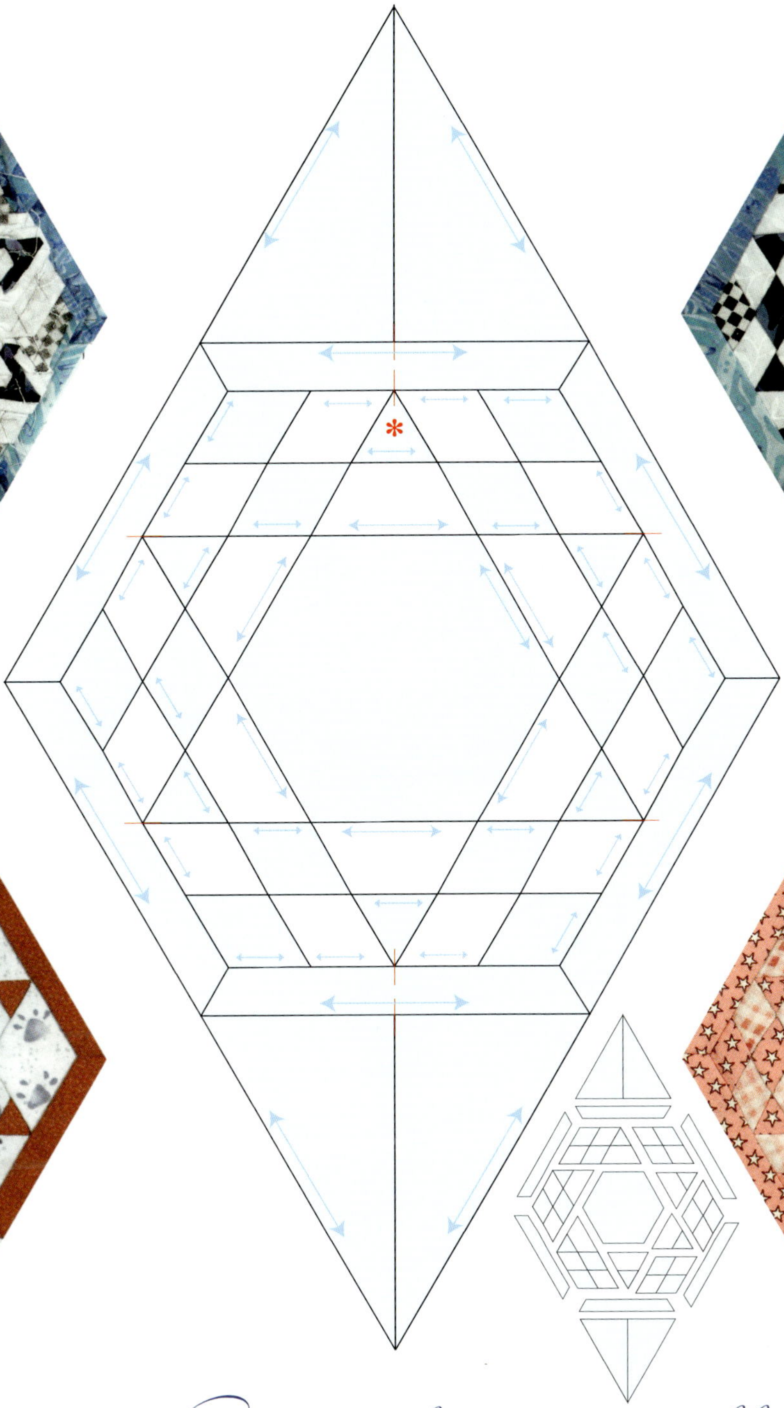

Never had any week passed so quickly.

(S&S Ch 19) Edward remained a week at the cottage;
he was earnestly pressed by Mrs. Dashwood to stay longer.

Tiny * pieces like these do not need to be on straight grain. You can eliminate seam lines when you trace the diamond onto freezer paper or print from Electric Quilt.

When the seam allowances are pressed *around* the intersections, even a diamond with this many pieces lies flat. Trimming is important to reduce the bulk.

Linda Franz

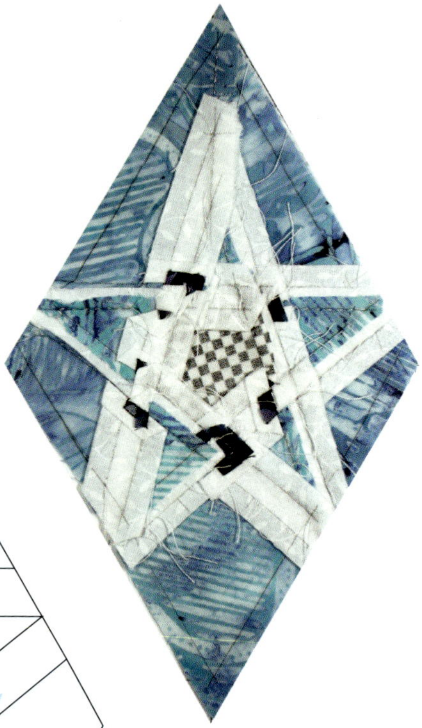

58

This is delightful, is not it?

(E Ch 38) Miss Bates and Miss Fairfax, escorted by two gentlemen, walked into the room...
"Well! This is brilliant indeed! This is admirable! Excellently contrived, upon my word.
Nothing wanting. Could not have imagined it. So well lighted up."

Choice is delightful, *is not it?* Two fabrics, six fabrics or seven fabrics? with 31 pieces or 21 pieces? If you eliminate seams, remember to replace them with matches.

Tiny interior * pieces do not need to be cut on straight grain and that makes the preparation go a little faster.

Which could hardly be seen without delight.

(S&S Ch 10) *Marianne was still handsomer....and in her eyes, which were very dark, there was a life, a spirit, an eagerness which could hardly be seen without delight.*

This diamond has tight curves. You may find it easier with the curved seam allowances cut slightly narrower than ¼ inch.

Mark matches every ¼ inch or so on curves and clip twice between the matches. For more tips on curves, see page 123 and the DVD lesson.

60

An air of good sense.

(P Ch 12) *The future owner of Kellynch was undoubtedly a gentleman,
and had an air of good sense.*

Purple and red? The choice of a mature quilter, with or without *an air of good sense*. Compare the front and back of the turquoise diamond to see the effect of mirror image.

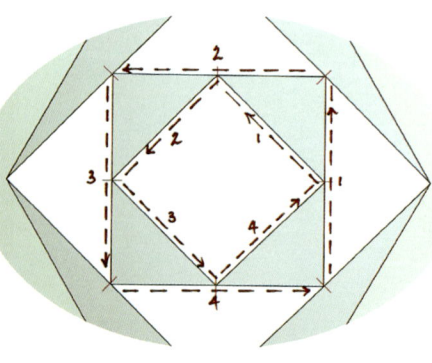

This design is quick and easy with continuous stitching and is ideal for a little "fussy cutting."

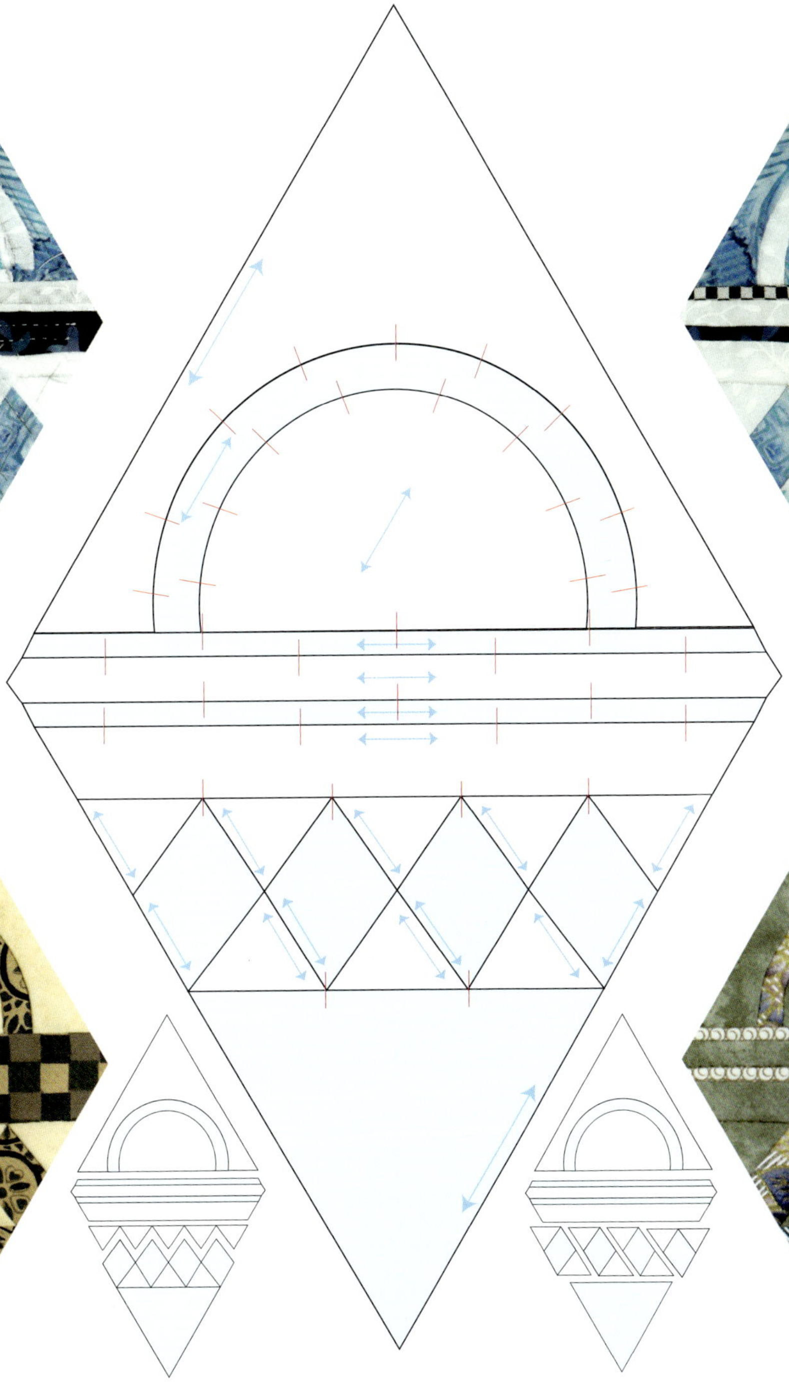

61

No greater delight than in making a filigree basket.

(S&S Ch 23) *"You are very good, I hope it won't hurt your eyes—
will you ring the bell for some working candles? My poor little girl would be
sadly disappointed, I know, if the basket was not finished tomorrow."*

In the brown and gold version, there
are fewer pieces but it looks just as
detailed thanks to the checkerboard
fabric.

Whether you stitch continuous
seams or stitch the pieces in rows,
the seams will press nicely, radiating
around the intersections.

62

Pleasanter demands

(P Ch 21) "It is really very good of you to come and sit with me,
when you must have so many pleasanter demands upon your time."

Mark matches every ¼ inch or so on tight curves and clip twice between the matches. For more about stitching curves see page 123 and the DVD lesson.

Three seams can radiate or fan around an intersection, just like four or more can, as shown here.

Quilted Diamonds 2

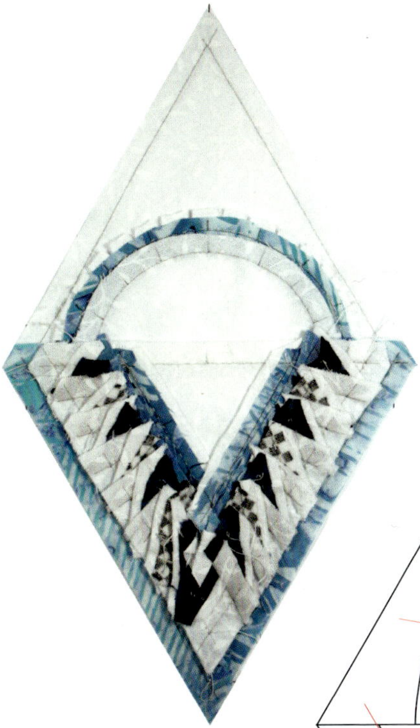

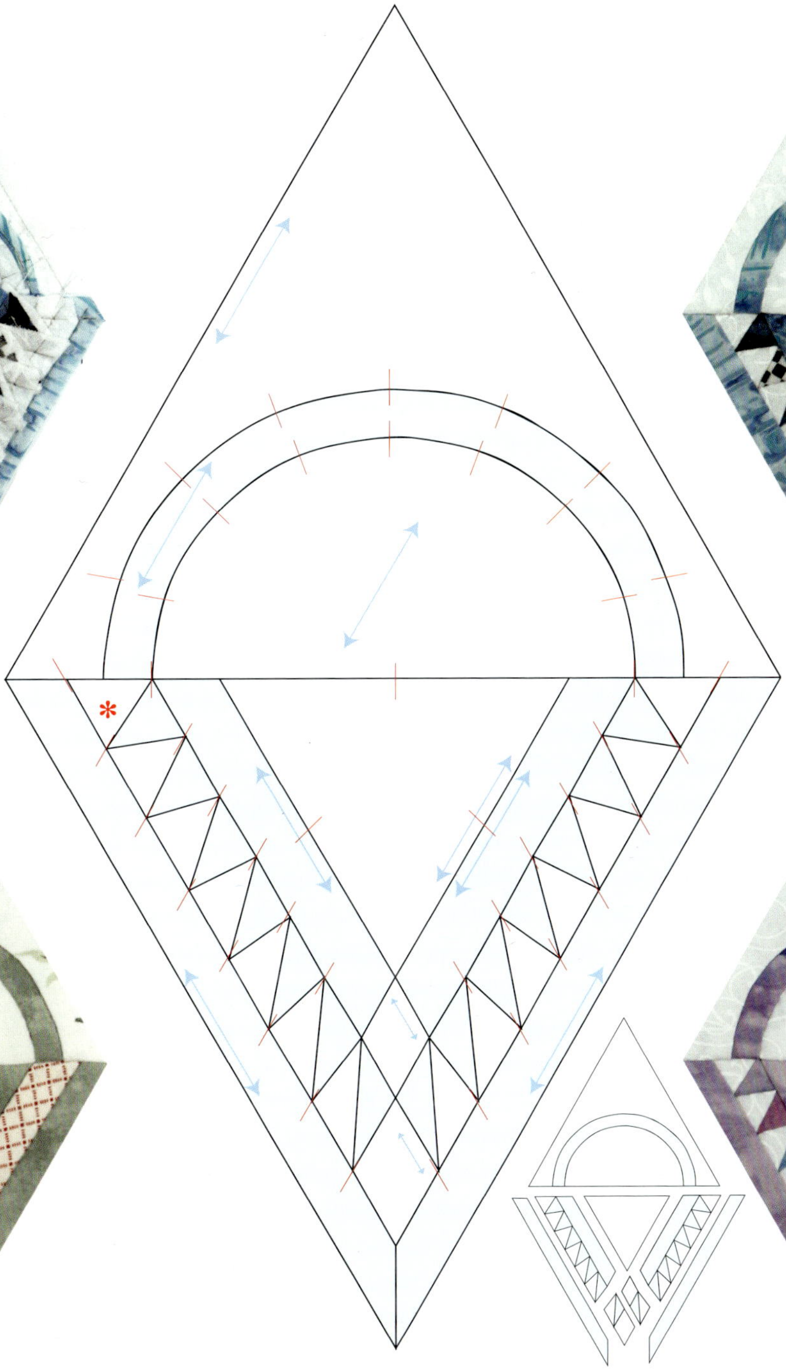

63

A source of felicity unknown before.

(P&P Ch 7) At present, indeed, they were well supplied both with news and happiness
by the recent arrival of a militia regiment in the neighborhood; ...This opened...a source of felicity unknown before.

The little triangles ***** do not need to be cut on straight grain and can be sewn with one thread, turning at every point, as shown for diamond #4 on the DVD. Also see page 122.

You may decide to simplify this diamond, as I did, by replacing the row of triangles with one piece. If you do, mark a few matches on the long seams.

64

An exclamation of delight.

(S&S Ch 26) *Marianne sat in silence almost all the way, wrapt in her own meditations, ...*
except when any object of picturesque beauty within their view drew from her an exclamation of delight.

Use matches and crosshairs when you pin, and pin one match at a time. Extra pins will catch your thread and might scratch your hands.

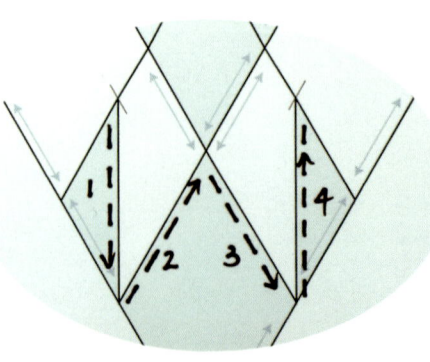

Four seams joining five pieces on each corner can be stitched continuously with one thread.

Quilted Diamonds 2

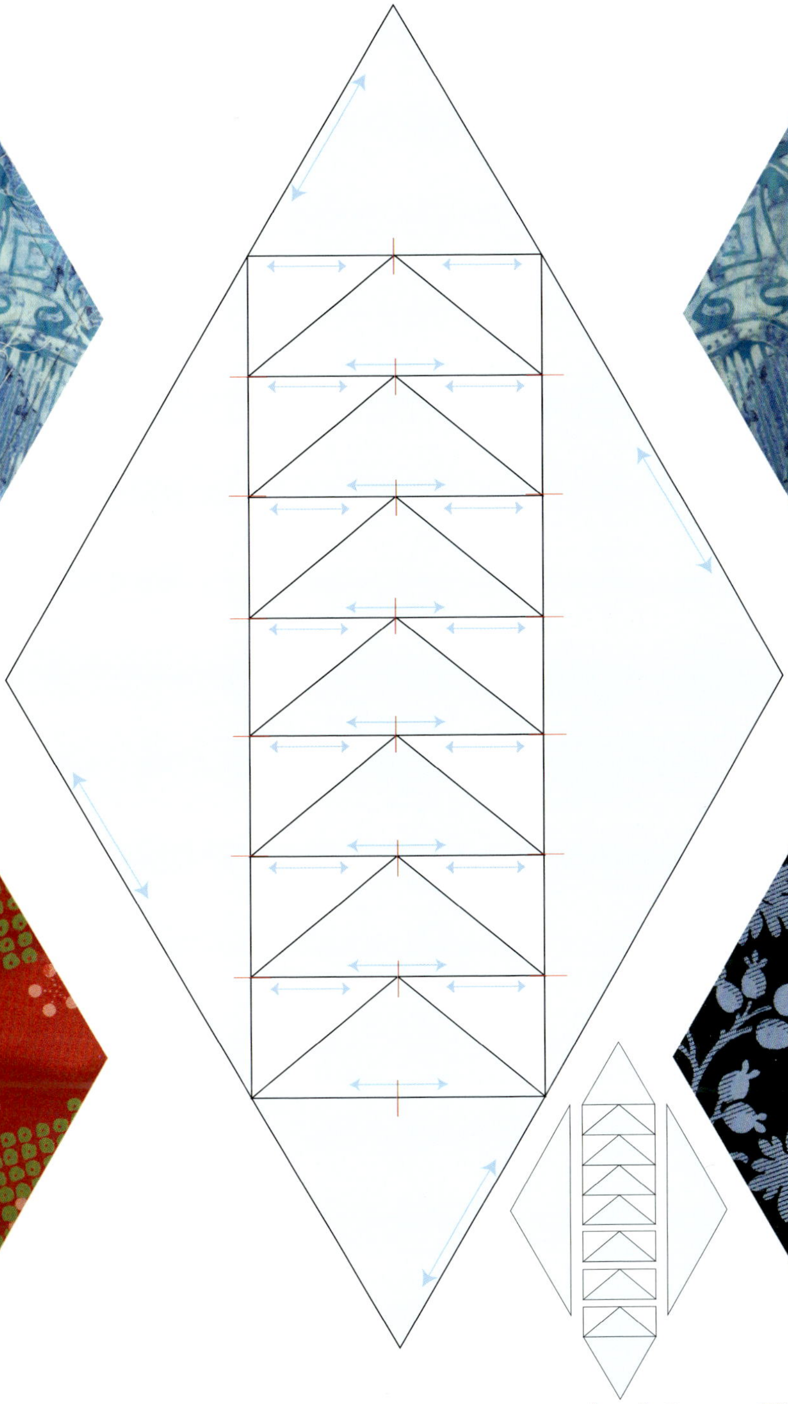

One day in the country is exactly like another.

(NA Ch 10) "But certainly there is much more sameness in a country life than in a Bath life.
One day in the country is exactly like another." "Here you are in pursuit only of amusement all day long."

There is a little more variety in this diamond than in a week in the country, with two, three or four fabrics and a simpler version.

Cut off long points, leaving just ¼ inch seam allowance. Long points can catch your thread while you are stitching, so don't wait until the diamond is finished to trim them.

66

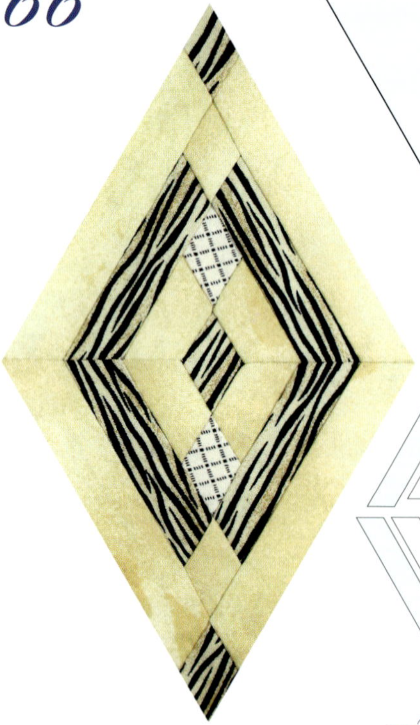

This will be complete enjoyment.

*(E Ch 36) We have the agreeable prospect of frequent visits from Frank the whole spring
—precisely the season of the year which one should have chosen for it; days always at the longest;
weather genial and pleasant, always inviting one out, and never too hot for exercise.*

Use matches and crosshairs when you are pinning. Precision can be a *complete enjoyment!* Pass the needle through crossing seam allowances.

If it is difficult to thread the needle, try a larger size. A #10 is longer than a #12 and has a larger eye. Try using an extra needle as a pin.

Quilted Diamonds 2

Have you a stout heart?

(NA Ch 20) "Will not your mind misgive you, when you find yourself in this gloomy chamber—too lofty and extensive for you, with only the feeble rays of a single lamp to take in its size—its walls hung with tapestry... and the bed...presenting even a funereal appearance. Will not your heart sink within you?"

Monkey was very disappointed that the fabrics in the dark paisley diamond did not have greater contrast.

For tips on joining seams with many seams converging, see page 123 and the DVD lesson.

68

The tea things were brought in.

(S&S Ch 26) Elinor and Marianne *reached town by three o'clock the third day, glad to be released, after such a journey, from the confinement of a carriage, and ready to enjoy all the luxury of a good fire.*

Forty pieces! Here is another opportunity for continuous stitching. Five small pieces can be joined with one thread for four seams.

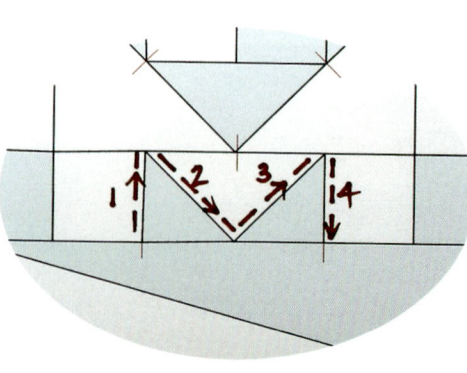

The simplified version has 29 pieces, with space for a teapot or other motif in the center. Add matches when you eliminate seams.

Quilted Diamonds 2

Georgiana's delight.

(P&P Ch 60) The joy which Miss Darcy expressed on receiving similar information, was as sincere as her brother's in sending it. Four sides of paper were insufficient to contain all her delight.

Stitch some curves with the clipped side up and some with the unclipped side up, facing you, to see which way you like better.

The simplified variation can be just as pretty, with only five pieces, and easy, gentle curves.

70

Clear, comprehensible, elegant English.

(P Ch 20) You have only knowledge enough of the language, to translate at sight these inverted, transposed, curtailed Italian lines, into clear, comprehensible, elegant English. You need not say anything more of your ignorance.—Here is complete proof.

Fifty-three pieces, anyone? Or maybe twenty-nine? If you decide to simplify this one, like I did, add matches where you eliminate seams to help you pin the seams.

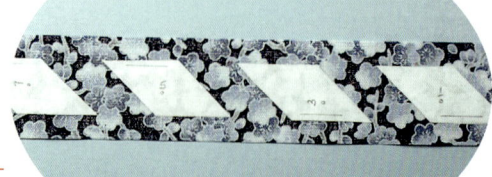

For tiny interior * pieces, it is not necessary to cut on straight grain. The rotary cutting goes fast when so many pieces can nest together, as demonstrated in the DVD lesson.

Quilted Diamonds 2

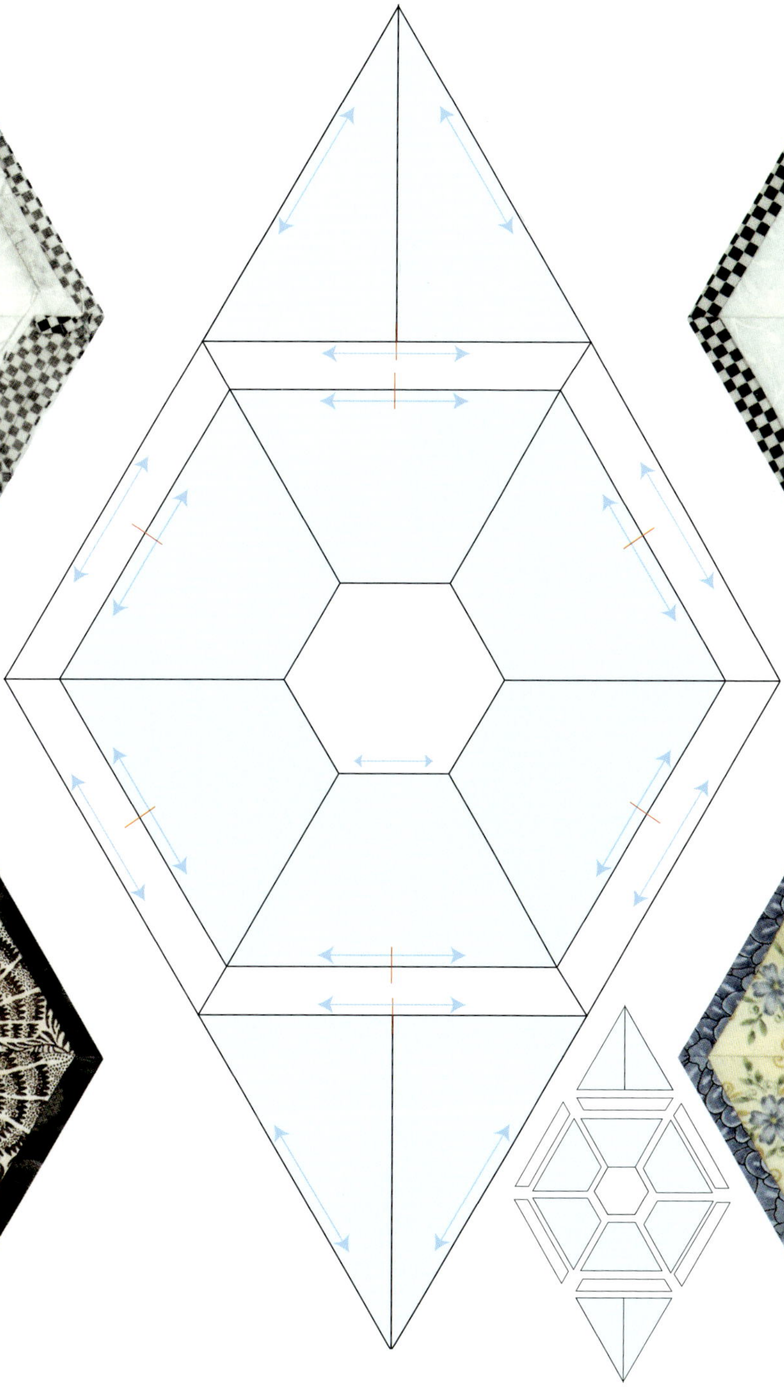

A good house and the liberty of the manor.

(P&P Ch 4) Mr. Bingley inherited property to the amount of nearly an hundred thousand pounds from his father, who had intended to purchase an estate, but did not live to do it.—Mr. Bingley intended it likewise.

Don't worry about pressing to the dark. The seams can be trimmed to eliminate shadowing and to reduce the bulk. When the seam allowances radiate around the intersections this well, the diamond lies flat and is easy to quilt, despite the number of pieces. The two "extra" vertical seams allow you to have straight grain on all of the outside edges.

The brilliancy of an unclouded night.

(MP Ch 11) All that was solemn and soothing, and lovely, appeared in the brilliancy of an unclouded night, and the contrast of the deep shade of the woods.

Whether two fabrics, four fabrics or seven fabrics, each fabric you choose should be tightly woven and press well.

All of the star points can be stitched continuously, turning a corner at every point, like the little triangles in diamond #4, demonstrated in the DVD lesson. See also page 122.

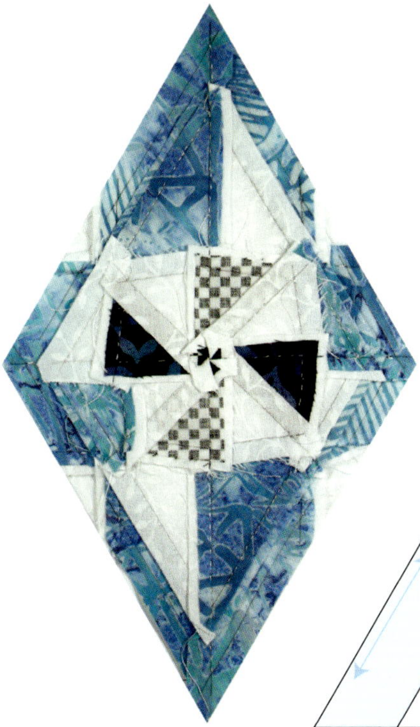

73

The sweets of friendship.

*(NA Ch 5) Here Catherine and Isabella, arm in arm,
again tasted the sweets of friendship in an unreserved conversation.*

You might like to "circle the intersection" when you join two halves of this diamond, as on page 123, and as demonstrated in the DVD lesson.

Lightly press the seam allowances around the center in one direction and then in the other. Sometimes one direction lines up better than the other.

Linda Franz

74

Exquisite, quite exquisite!

*(E Ch 29) "Miss Woodhouse, you have the art of giving pictures in a few words.
Exquisite, quite exquisite! ...May I hope for the honor of your hand for the two first dances
of this little projected ball, to be given...at the Crown Inn?"*

This exquisite design has multiple curves, insets, and many seams converging. I would not want to stitch this design on the sewing machine!

The curves all press toward the center of the diamond, but where they overlap, one seam must turn to lie back on itself, as shown.

Affectionate, open, artless, confiding.

(S&S Ch 44) The next morning brought another short note from Marianne—
still affectionate, open, artless, confiding—I could not answer it...
But I thought of her, I believe, every moment of the day.

If you forget to mark matches before you cut the pattern apart, you can add them later. There are tips for adding them in the DVD lesson.

Some seam allowances will press in a radiating manner and others should be pressed to the side with the fewest seams.

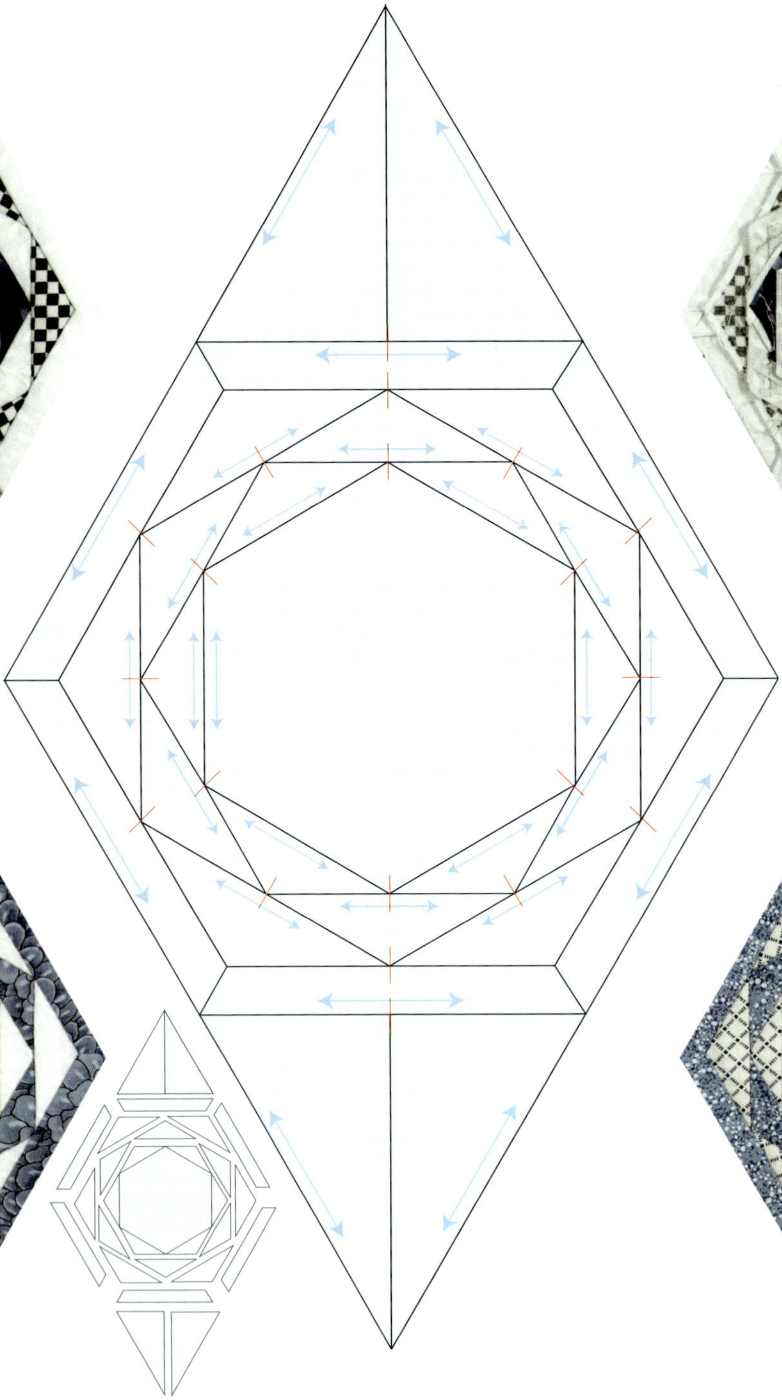

76

It was but an effusion of lively spirits.

(E Ch 24) He argued like a young man very much bent on dancing...
He seemed to have all the life and spirit, cheerful feelings, and social inclinations of his father.

The hexagon in the center is a nice opportunity to "fussy cut" a flower or a monkey or another element in the fabric design.

Although I normally piece with a neutral, light-colored thread, I try to match the fabric when stitching seams where both fabrics are darker.

It was just occupation enough.

(P Ch 20) Anne's mind was in a most favorable state for the entertainment of the evening:
it was just occupation enough: she had feelings for the tender, spirits for the gay...and patience for the wearisome.

This is one of my favorites for "fussy cutting." It presses well and there is no need to cut the tiny interior pieces * on straight grain.

All thread is not the same. If you thread the fresh cut, and knot the other end, you may find it tangles less. If not, try knotting the freshly cut end.

Linda Franz

78

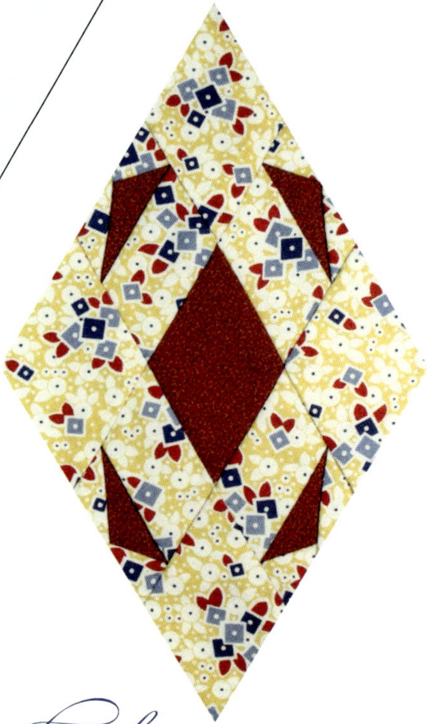

You cannot think I shall leave off matchmaking.

(E Ch 1) I promise you to make none for myself, papa; but I must, indeed, for other people.
It is the greatest amusement in the world!

Continuous stitching possibilities
and there is even a simpler variation
—easy to piece precisely with
matching marks. *You cannot think I
shall leave off matchmaking!*

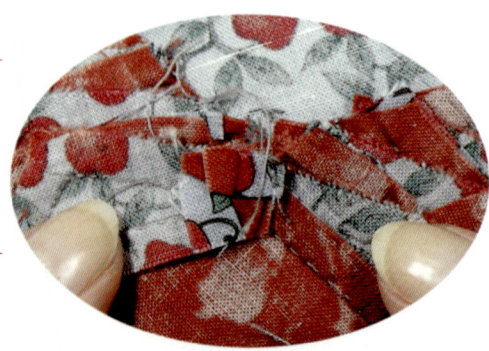

I carry reading glasses in my sewing
kit. Consider wearing stronger
glasses when you quilt, or using a
larger needle, to make it easier to
thread the needle.

Quilted Diamonds 2

A rational creature speaking the truth from her heart.

(P&P Ch 19) "I do assure you, Sir, that I have no pretension whatever to the kind of elegance
which consists in tormenting a respectable man. I would rather be paid the compliment of being believed sincere."

My sister, Alison Murchie, stitched
the turquoise diamond for me. It had
to be one named for Miss Elizabeth
Bennet of *Pride and Prejudice!*

There is only one other diamond in
the book that I did not stitch myself.

Linda Franz

80

A most attractive picture of happiness.

*(P Ch 18) The Crofts brought with them their country habit of being almost always together.
He was ordered to walk, to keep off the gout, and Mrs. Croft seemed to go shares with him in everything,
and to walk for her life, to do him good. Anne saw them wherever she went.*

The 16 pieces in the border of this diamond can be stitched continuously with one thread, if you like, and then added to the center.

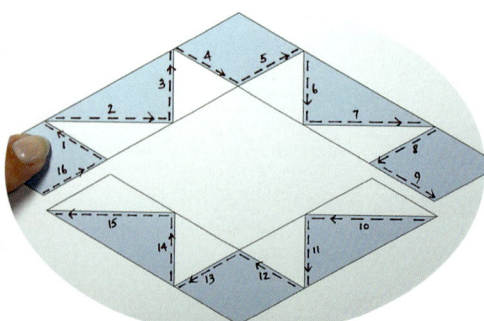

By eliminating the seams in the center, you can create a space for "fussy cutting" and reduce the number of pieces from 37 to 17.

Quilted Diamonds 2

A considerable hoard of diamonds.

(NA Ch 20) Impelled by an irresistible presentiment, you will eagerly advance to it, unlock its folding doors,
and search into every drawer;—but for some time without discovering anything of importance
—perhaps nothing but a considerable hoard of diamonds.

Sew the diamonds together in diagonal rows, as in the little diagram, or piece continuously turning corners at the points. Matches guarantee precision!

The simpler variation has 21 pieces instead of 33. Either way, some seam allowances radiate well and others press behind the narrow bands.

Linda Franz

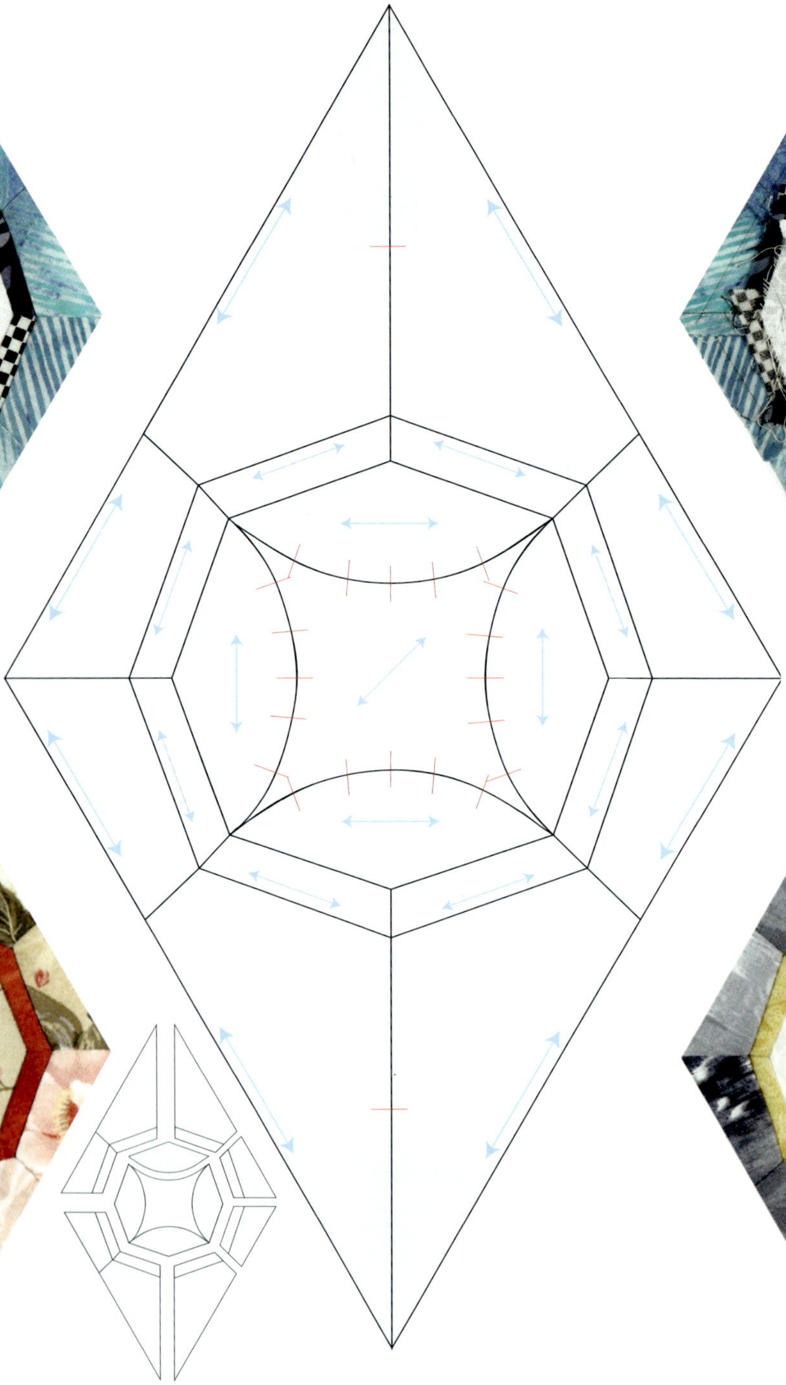

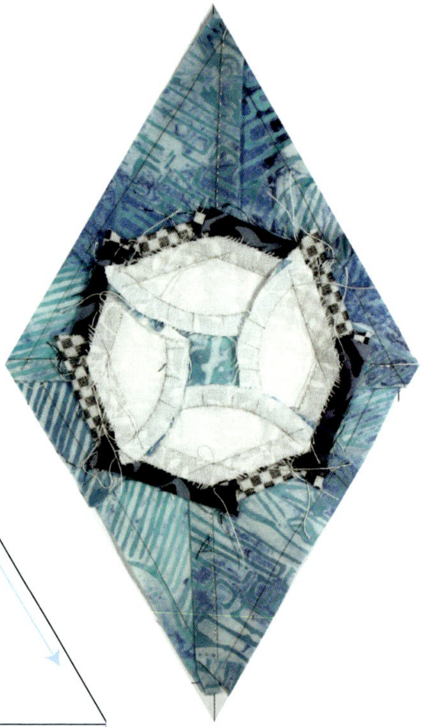

82

The young people were all wild to see Lyme.

(P Ch 11) *They were consequently to stay the night there,
and not to be expected back till the next day's dinner.*

I was quite happy with these
diamonds until I decided to try
pressing one with steam.

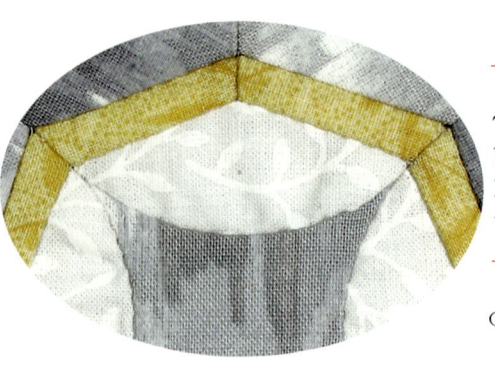

The ripples in the gray diamond will
be less noticeable when quilted, but
Monkey says, "Boo boo. Don't do
that again!"

It was a beautiful evening, mild and still.

(MP Ch 10) It was a beautiful evening, mild and still,
and the drive was as pleasant as the serenity of nature could make it.

You can join all the pieces in the two borders with the star points by continuous stitching (as in diamond #80), or in the same order you would use for machine piecing.

You can simplify the border, as I did in the green and gold version, and know that this diamond will still look good in two, three or four fabrics.

84

Catherine felt herself in high luck.

(NA Ch 3) They made their appearance in the Lower Rooms; and here fortune was more favorable to our heroine.
The master of the ceremonies introduced to her a very gentlemanlike young man.

Press the seams in a radiating manner (counterclockwise or clockwise) around one intersection. Some seam allowances are then committed for the adjacent ones.

There are 28 pieces in 14 square inches—but this diamond is light and flat when it is finished, pressed and trimmed, and is not difficult to quilt. Don't forget to trim (page 125).

85

With her usual cheerfulness.

(S&S Ch 25) Mrs. Dashwood *insisted on their both accepting Mrs. Jennings' invitation directly,
and then began to foresee with her usual cheerfulness, a variety of advantages
that would accrue to them all, from this separation.*

The pieces in the center are small but don't worry—they look a little bigger with the seam allowances, so you have something to hold on to!

Choose your fabric with care. Thick, loosely woven fabrics are not suitable for these small pieces. Why not combine a batik and a fine, high quality cotton?

Linda Franz

86

Enough to catch any man's heart.

(MP Ch 7) *A young woman, pretty, lively, with a harp as elegant as herself; and both placed near a window, cut down to the ground, and opening on a little lawn...was enough to catch any man's heart.*

Press the seams in a radiating manner when you can and toward the outside (toward the pieces with the fewest seams) to distribute the bulk.

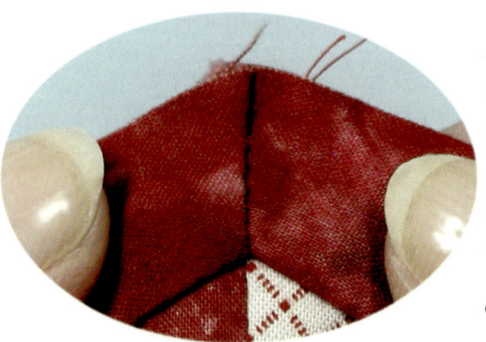

Although I normally piece with a single strand of neutral colored thread, I switched to a matching red for the mitered borders in this diamond.

Nothing could be more delightful.

(P&P Ch 3) *He was quite young, wonderfully handsome, extremely agreeable...Nothing could be more delightful! To be fond of dancing was a certain step towards falling in love; and very lively hopes of Mr. Bingley's heart were entertained.*

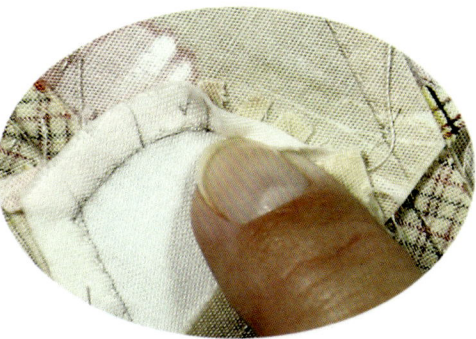

You may find this easier to stitch if you cut the curved seam allowances slightly narrower than ¼ inch. Mark more matches where the curve is tightest and clip *between* the matches, rather than *at* the matches, so when you pin you have something to ease. See page 123 and the DVD lesson for more tips on curves.

Linda Franz

88

You know the ease, and the pleasure with which this would be done.

(MP Ch 42) *I will immediately come down, and take you back to Mansfield.*

When joining two halves of a diamond with many seams converging, you might want to "circle the intersection," as shown on page 123 and in the DVD lesson.

Lightly press the seams around the center in one direction, and then the other. Sometimes the intersection matches better in one direction than the other.

Quilted Diamonds 2

89

A bewitching charm.

(P Ch 11) There was...such a bewitching charm in a degree of hospitality so uncommon, so unlike the usual style of give-and-take invitations, and dinners of formality and display... "These would have been all my friends."

This diamond has many very short seams which can be stitched with just one load of the needle, in a comfortable rhythm, taking 5 or 6 stitches at a time.

Use the matches to ensure that all of the bars line up perfectly. There is *a bewitching charm* for me in this kind of precision!

Linda Franz

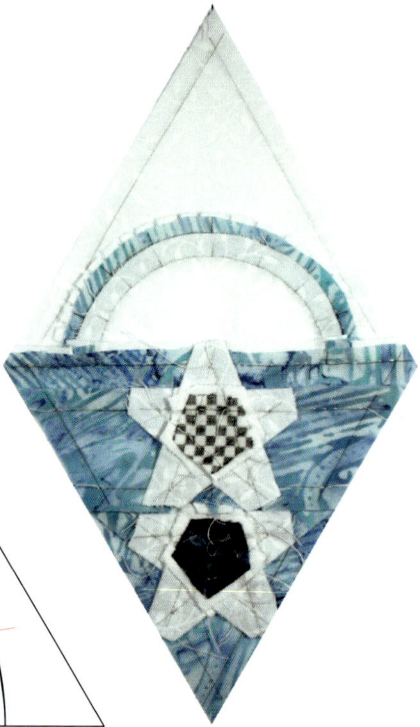

90

Elizabeth's spirits soon rising to playfulness.

(P&P Ch 60) Elizabeth's spirits soon rising to playfulness again, she wanted Mr. Darcy to account for his having ever fallen in love with her. "How could you begin?" said she.

You may ignore suggested grain on tiny * pieces. The matches make it much easier to stitch this diamond design, especially on the curves.

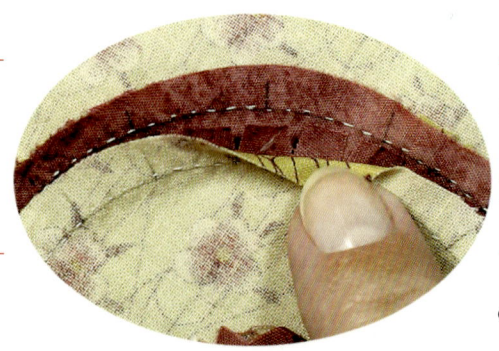

Five-pointed stars are often associated with the flag of our American friends. Maybe my next version will be red, white and blue!

Quilted Diamonds 2

91

Absolutely plain—but extremely elegant and amiable.

*(E Ch 19) Mrs. Dixon, I understand, has no remarkable degree of personal beauty; is not, by any means,
to be compared with Miss Fairfax...Miss Campbell always was absolutely plain—but extremely elegant and amiable.*

Don't worry about pressing to the dark. By trimming the dark seam allowances a scant 1/8 inch, you can avoid shadowing and eliminate bulk, so the diamond looks its best.

Here is another nice opportunity for "fussy cutting" a design from the fabric. The four triangles can be added to the center square without breaking the thread.

92

Elegance, propriety, regularity, harmony

(MP Ch 39) The elegance, propriety, regularity, harmony—and perhaps, above all, the peace and tranquility of Mansfield, were brought to her remembrance every hour of the day.

Notice the effect of mirror image, where the placement of colors on the back is the opposite on the front. This always happens, because we iron freezer paper templates onto the

wrong side of the fabric, but we only notice it when the designs are not symmetrical. See page 118.

Two versions again—your choice!

The day was bright, her courage high.

(NA Ch 24) *In the course of this morning's reflections,*
she came to a resolution of making her next attempt on the forbidden door alone.

When many seams converge in the middle like this, there are some simple strategies to make sure your diamond lies flat.

See page 123 and the DVD lesson for tips on "circling the intersection" and adding a third line inside the crosshairs.

Linda Franz

94

A very pretty amber cross.

(MP Ch 26) The almost solitary ornament in her possession, a very pretty amber cross which William had brought her from Sicily, was the greatest distress of all, for she had nothing but a bit of ribbon to fasten it to.

For tiny interior * pieces, it is not necessary to cut on straight grain. That can speed up the rotary cutting. Add more matches, if you like.

The wide border is a nice place to showcase a fabric with a larger design. Even after it is pressed and trimmed, the center of this one will be thick to quilt.

Quilted Diamonds 2

95

An air of decided fashion.

(P&P Ch 3) Mr. Bingley was good looking and gentlemanlike;
...His sisters were fine women, with an air of decided fashion.

You may decide to appliqué the basket handle but these curves are easy to hand piece and will press well with the little clips lying open.

If your thread is tangling, try using shorter lengths. Some brands of thread have a nap, and if you drag it through the fabric against the nap, it is more likely to tangle.

96

The wind roared down the chimney.

(NA Ch 21) *She paused a moment in breathless wonder. The wind roared down the chimney,
the rain beat in torrents against the windows, and everything seemed to speak the awfulness of her situation.*

This looks very different in two turquoise variations. Matches are helpful when attaching the four borders.

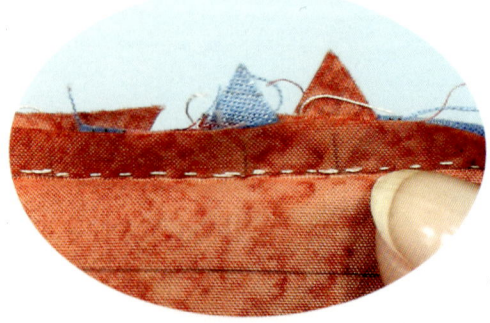

Do not use the last 3 or 4 inches of thread to eke out a seam! It has been dragged through the fabric too many times and is worn.

Quilted Diamonds 2

97

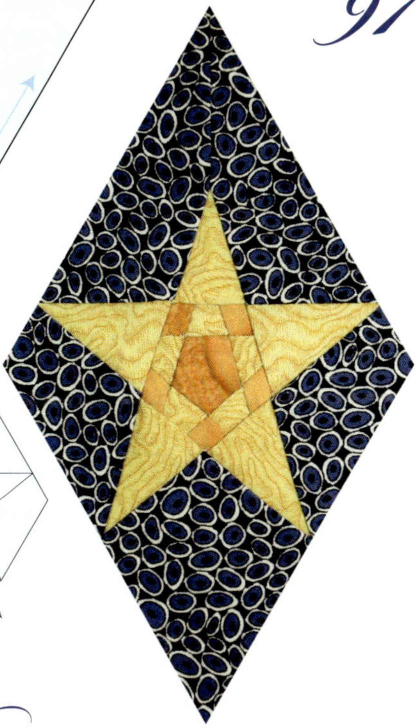

Five daughters brought up at home.

(P&P Ch 29) "No governess! How was that possible?
Five daughters brought up at home without a governess!—I never heard of such a thing."

Tiny interior * pieces like these do not need to be cut on straight grain. This design can not be sewn well with a coarse, loosely woven fabric!

You may have wondered about the reference to Preparation H on the DVD. I use the cream on sore quilting fingers. It really works!

98

I have pleasure in many things.

(P&P Ch 8) "I deserve neither such praise nor such censure," cried Elizabeth;
"I am not a great reader, and I have pleasure in many things."

When I cut out the chooks, I worked with a larger piece of fabric, rather than the strips I normally use.

I ignored straight grain when necessary to catch a chook. Thanks to the mitered borders there is straight grain on all of the outside edges of this diamond.

Quilted Diamonds 2

She had nothing more to wish for.

(MP Ch 28) *"You must dance with me, Fanny; you must keep two dances for me; any two that you like, except the first." She had nothing more to wish for.*

If you have something *more to wish for*, you could simplify this diamond and create a space for "fussy cutting" in the middle.

Other than the center intersection, you will probably want to press all of the seams outward—toward the pieces with the fewest seams.

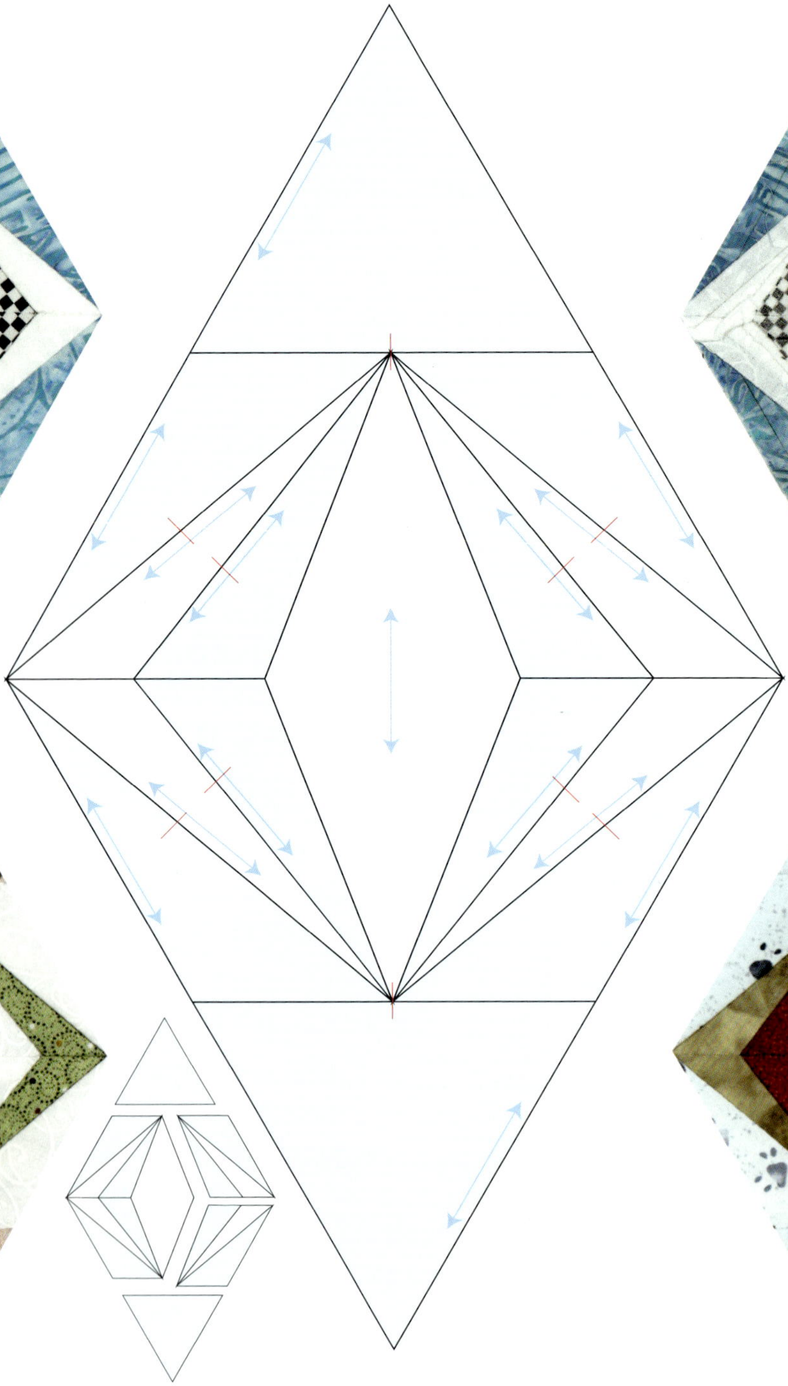

100

This was so thoughtful and kind.

(MP Ch 3) —and would he only have smiled upon her and called her "my dear Fanny," while he said it
every former frown or cold address might have been forgotten. Fanny is starved for affection at Mansfield.

Add a third line at the edge of the
freezer paper, inside the normal
crosshair, on sharp points, as on
page 123, or compensate "by eye" to
make pieces fit better,

It is a good idea to slide the needle
along the thread slightly when
you pull through, so the eye of the
needle does not cause wear in one
place.

Quilted Diamonds 2

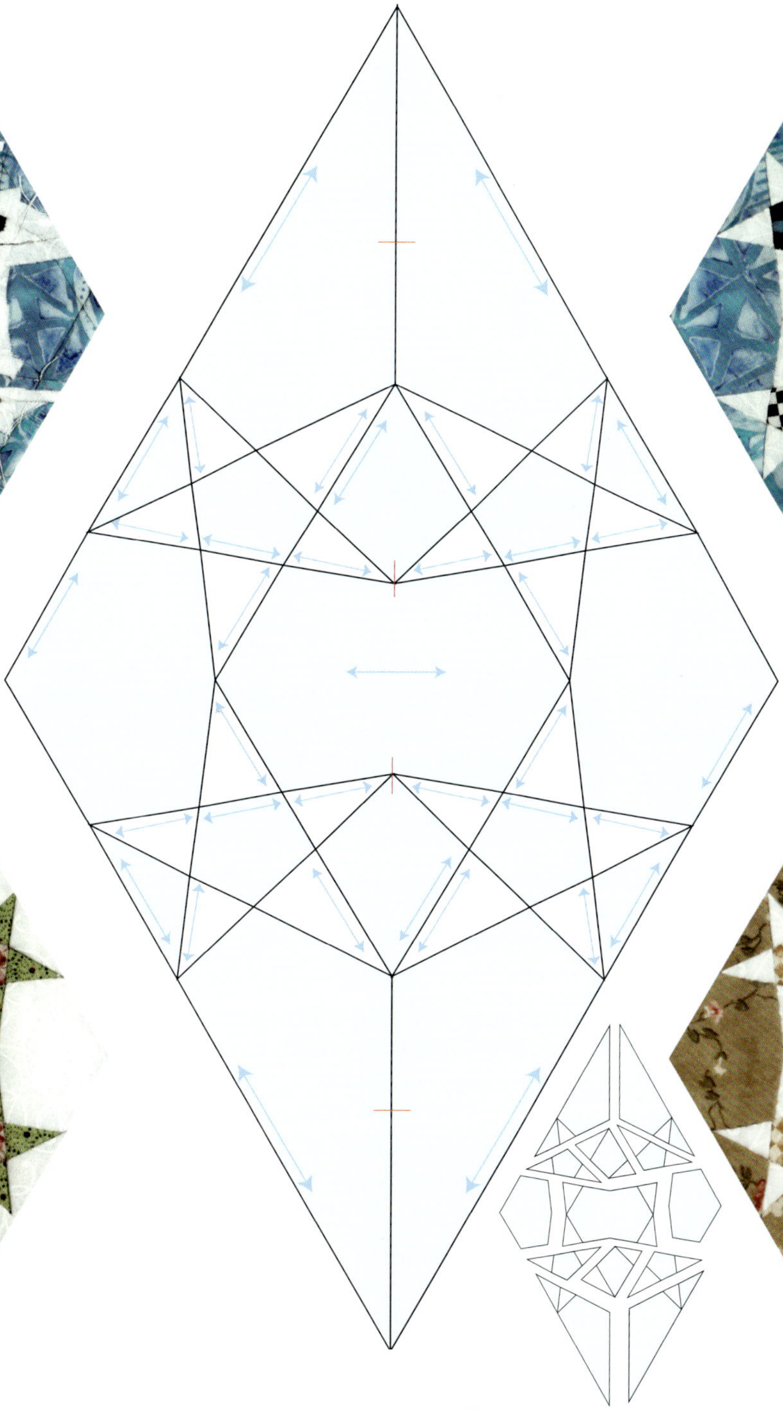

Elizabeth could not but smile at such a conclusion of such a beginning.

(P&P Ch 20) "An unhappy alternative is before you, Elizabeth. From this day you must be a stranger to one of your parents.—Your mother will never see you again if you do not marry Mr. Collins, and I will never see you again if you do."

We conclude the way we began, with five-pointed stars. This star is often used as a symbol of freedom, reminding us that freezer paper templates give us freedom to draw whatever designs we like—and cut them apart and sew them together!

The quotation comes from one of the funniest scenes in the novel.

fabric

4 fabrics

3 fabrics

2 fabrics

Look for contrast, and choose from quality cotton fabrics that press well and do not fray easily. Buy the best fabric you can afford.

Your diamonds will look best in cotton fabrics that retain their interest in tiny pieces. All of the fabrics should be similar weight.

A fabric that frays easily or that does not press well will be frustrating, no matter how careful you are.

Can you see pencil lines on the wrong side?

I like working with batiks, and other fine, cool, quality cotton fabrics. Raiding my stash for 202 of the 303 diamonds in this book was *a constant source of delight![7]* I don't hesitate to cut into my favorite fabrics because a diamond uses so little!

For this hand piecing technique, we stitch along a marked line, rather than following the cut edge of the fabric to make our ¼ inch seams, so it is important to be able to see a fine pencil line on the wrong side. Many dark fabrics are light enough on the wrong side to pass the pencil test, and there are other strategies you can use if the dark fabric you love requires special treatment (page 116) but *consider whether the inconvenience of it might not very much exceed the pleasure.[8]*

I prefer to wash all of my fabric before I put it in my stash. I want to test for color fastness (see DVD), and preshrink the fabric. If I have bought a whole bolt for a big quilt, I just wash one or two yards at a time, rather than washing and ironing it all at once.

Even if you don't normally wash your fabric before using it, you might want to wash it for your hand piecing projects. The freezer paper will stick more easily, and the fabric will feel softer and silkier in your hands while you are stitching.

scrappy diamonds	some diamonds can be made from 2 contrasting scraps only 6 x 6 inches
30 diamonds in 2 fabrics	a generous rule of thumb is to allow 1 to 1 ¼ yards of each fabric
28 plain setting diamonds	allow ½ yard or more
Love & Friendship (queen) 84 x 92 inches	approximately 8 ½ yards of the blue focus fabric and 9 ½ yards of the white This includes sashing, cornerstones, setting diamonds and binding, but does not include the fabric on the back of the quilt.

It is important to have straight grain on the outside edges of any quilt block, square or diamond, whenever possible. It is more stable and less likely to distort. Your quilt top will be easier to assemble and will lie flat.

Suggested grain line is marked on the patterns. Straight grain is not as critical on interior pieces, and very small pieces (some of which are marked *) need not be cut on straight grain.

Lengthwise grain has very little stretch, crosswise grain has a little more stretch, and true bias at 45 degrees is very stretchy. You may use either crosswise or lengthwise grain for straight grain.

When a diamond does have bias on the outside edges, be careful not to stretch it out of shape. Try not to handle bias more than necessary, and never use steam to press it.

All of these steps are demonstrated in the DVD lesson.

1. Trace the diamond onto freezer paper, using a thin, flexible ruler and a mechanical pencil.

2. Number each piece on the master and the freezer paper, so you can tell where the pieces belong when they are cut apart.

3. Indicate which fabric each piece is to be cut from, allowing for mirror image, if necessary. (See page 118 and the DVD.)

4. Mark grain line on each piece, as indicated on the pattern.

5. Mark matches to assist in pinning the seams accurately.

6. Cut the freezer paper pieces apart.

making templates
with freezer paper

For each pattern, you will need to transfer the design onto freezer paper to make templates.

How did our quilting ancestors make do without plastic coated freezer paper! It has many advantages over other kinds of template material. *It appears to me the most desirable arrangement in the world.*[9]

It is worth the time to make these templates because they can be used over and over and over again. I used some of mine about 30 times each when I cut the 240 sashing strips for Love & Friendship.

Freezer paper is semi-transparent, so you can trace your pattern. Almost anything you can draw, you can turn into templates. It allows you to concentrate on the design, not measurements, because you don't need to consider seam allowances until you cut out the fabric pieces. That creates incredible design freedom.

You can print onto freezer paper, instead of tracing, with an inkjet printer (NOT laser!), or print onto adhesive labels, if you have Electric Quilt and a *Quilted Diamonds CD.* (See page 128 and the DVD.)

Whatever size or shape the freezer paper, you just add ¼ inch seam allowances when you cut the fabric. There is no elaborate measuring and math.

For diamonds, I like to work with little rolls of freezer paper 4½ inches wide, as on the DVD. I get four rolls from 18 inch wide freezer paper.

Freezer paper templates are ironed onto the wrong side of the fabric for hand piecing, so they always produce the mirror image of the pattern. (See page 118 and the DVD.) You might want to take this into consideration when you mark which fabric is to be used for each piece. If you are printing from the optional *QD2 CD,* you can print in color, and set your printer options for "mirror image."

When ironing freezer paper, use a hot, dry iron. No steam! If your pieces are not sticking, your iron is not hot enough. You might like to use a Teflon ironing board cover, or iron on a hard surface like a wooden bread board covered with aluminum foil, so the freezer paper will stick better.

ironing the templates

On your ironing surface, you should have scissors for rough cuts, a second ruler, a strip of colored paper cut exactly ½ inch wide, a toothpick, and some chocolate.

The iron should be on cotton setting, no steam. Freezer paper will always stick better to fabrics that have been washed. Spray starch or sizing may prevent the freezer paper from sticking well.

HOT TIP: If your freezer paper does not adhere well, it may be that your iron is not hot enough. To compensate, iron the pieces on a hard surface like a wooden bread board covered with aluminum foil, or on a Teflon ironing board cover.

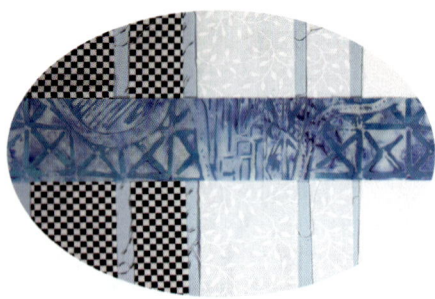

Try working with fabric strips cut in several widths. It is more convenient, saves waste, and makes the rotary cutting easier. See the DVD for tips about strip width.

The templates are all the finished size, so we need to leave room for the seam allowances when we space the pieces on the wrong side of the fabric.

I space the pieces on the wrong side with the ½ inch strip of colored paper, so I know I will have enough room for two ¼ inch seam allowances, without waste.

Often the pieces nest together so you can make one cut and get two perfect ¼ inch seam allowances. As you can see on the DVD, the cutting goes fast!

For small *interior* pieces, you may decide to ignore the suggested grain line and place the piece to have a flower or other element of the print fabric "fussy cut" for effect.

You might like to steady tiny pieces with a toothpick, rather than risking your finger near a hot iron. A friend suggested attaching a button so it is easier to pick up.

rotary cutting

Our quilting ancestors used scissors and probably learned very young to cut a ¼ inch seam allowance by eye.

I only use scissors to cut curves and deep insets. I prefer to use a rotary cutter. It gives an absolutely accurate ¼ inch seam and it is fast. You can see how fast on the DVD!

 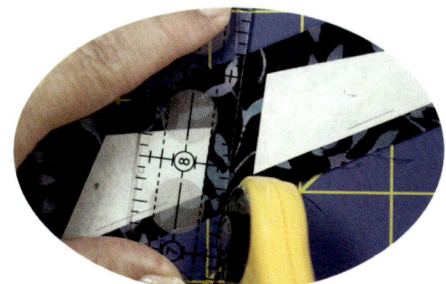 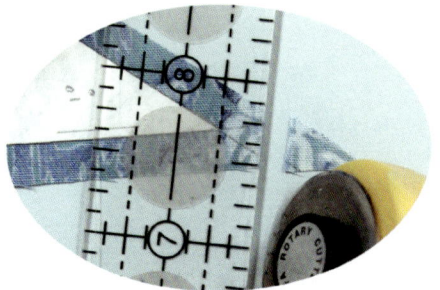

Cutting an exact ¼ inch seam is not essential because we stitch following a line, not the edge of the fabric, the way we do when we machine piece. However, it is satisfying to me to have the seam allowances line up, and rotary cutting is faster and easier than cutting with scissors.

There are many good rulers available for rotary cutting. Cut on an ordinary self-healing mat, or on one that rotates, and line up two lines of the ruler when you can.

Knock off any extra-long points when you notice them. You will trim the diamonds when they are finished, but in the meantime, long points can catch your thread and be inconvenient.

It was performed with suitable quietness and uneventful safety.[10]

ROTARY CUTTING SAFETY
(and don't tell Mr. Woodhouse)

Always use a very sharp blade because it is safer! When a blade becomes dull you need to press harder. This is dangerous because you have less control.

Never, ever, cut towards yourself!

Keep the cutter out of reach of children and teach them that it is dangerous to touch it.

Use the safety lock every time you put the cutter down. Make it a habit.

Cut with the handle at about a 45-degree angle to the board for maximum control.

Keep your cutter clean. It usually just needs a wipe with a scrap of fabric but occasionally you may need to disassemble it. If the cutter is gummed up with lint the blade will not turn easily, causing you to press harder. Again, this is dangerous because you have less control.

To allow the blade to turn easily, keep the nut just tight enough to secure the blade, not tightened all the way.

Always cut on the correct side of the ruler—right side for righties, left side for lefties.

Never use an ordinary thin ruler with the rotary cutter. Thick plastic rulers in appropriate sizes make rotary cutting easier and safer.

To work comfortably and safely, work with good lighting on a sturdy surface at the right height for you.

Keep your cutting mat clean and clear of clutter.

Try different brands and styles of cutters and rulers to find the ones that are right for you.

Linda Franz

marking seam lines

Switch back to a thin, flexible ruler to mark seam lines. Use a mechanical pencil with a fine lead and a light touch! You want to be able to see the line, but just. A heavy line will make your diamonds less accurate and can make your hands and fabric dirty. You can see this demonstrated on the DVD.

Align the ruler on top of the template to avoid loosening the freezer paper. This is a portable job, but it is easier with the fabric lying on a cutting mat or a very fine sandpaper surface. If the fabric drags under the pencil, it makes it more difficult to be accurate and loosens the freezer paper.

Extend the lines beyond the corners, so there are crosshairs to match at the seam endings. This makes it much easier to be precise. The accuracy of these lines will determine the accuracy of your diamonds, so take your time. *"If it's worth doing, it's worth doing right."* (A quotation from my parents!)

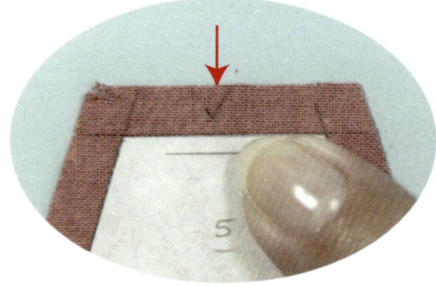

Matches make it easier to pin and stitch seams. There are suggested matches on each pattern, in red. Click on the DVD menu for tips on adding matches, if you forgot them.

If there is a danger of turning a piece top to bottom when the freezer paper is gone, you might like to mark the top seam allowance.

You may prefer to mark seam lines before cutting, but once the pieces are cut out, it is a portable project. If you run out of time, you can mark the seams lines on the go.

marking on dark fabrics

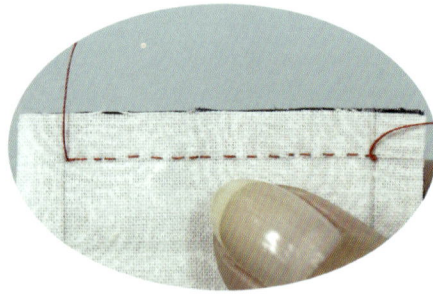

Use white, yellow or silver pencils or markers on dark fabrics. You will need a good sharpener to keep the pencil line as thin as possible.

Be careful to cut EXACT ¼ inch seam allowances on dark fabrics, so it is easier to judge ¼ inch, even when you cannot see the line at all.

If you hand piece with the lighter fabric up, facing you, the line on the darker fabric is not as important. Good lighting is a big asset!

Quilted Diamonds 2

sewing kits

"All her apparatus of happiness."[11]

Kit for prep

Kit for sewing on the go

You can easily carry these tools with you if you want to meet with friends to prepare diamonds. If you have a regular date to prepare diamonds you will always have something ready to stitch on the go.

I keep my sewing tools in a clear plastic bag and carry the master pattern and the prepared pieces in a plastic sheet protector. It is very portable and simple. You will probably want a separate set of tools for your travel kit.

needles

between

sharp

straw (milliner's)

I prefer a sharp, but you should try piecing with betweens or straws and decide for yourself. See the tips on the pattern pages and the DVD.

The most important thing to remember about your needle is that it is not a family heirloom! Treat yourself to a new needle often.

A needle is a wire covered with a very fine metal plating which wears away as we stitch. A needle might look good, but if the delicate finish is worn, it will not slide through the fabric as well as it should. Always dispose of a bent or dull needle right way.

thread

It is best to use 100% cotton thread with cotton fabric. Choose a color that matches your background fabric or your focus fabric, or use a neutral color that blends.

I cut my thread about 15 inches long and sew with a single strand.

All thread is not the same. Try different brands. It is amazing how much difference there can be between brands of cotton thread!

Hand piecers drag the thread through the fabric many times to make stitches, so the thread wears. There are more notes about thread on the pattern pages and the DVD.

threading

Threading the needle should not be a frustration in this pleasant, gentle sewing process. There are threading tips on the DVD and on the pattern pages in addition to these:

Cutting the thread at an angle makes it easier to thread. Thread several needles onto the spool before getting in the car!

Consider using a larger needle. A #10 is larger than a #12 and has a bigger eye.

Try holding the needle in the other hand, and move the needle towards the thread—or use a needle threader, as shown above.

sewing sequence

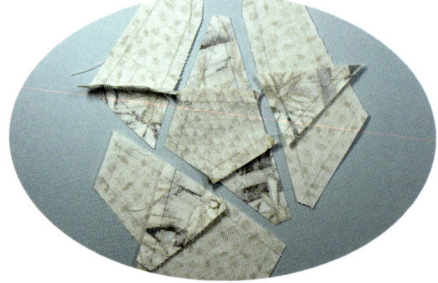

Lay the pieces out in the diamond shape, in order, *wrong side up* on your sewing surface using the numbering on your master pattern as a guide.

You can use the same approach you would use for machine piecing, looking for pieces that can be joined to form triangles, squares, diamonds and rows.

There is a small diagram with each pattern to give you a hint. There may be a number of other good sewing sequences in addition to the one shown.

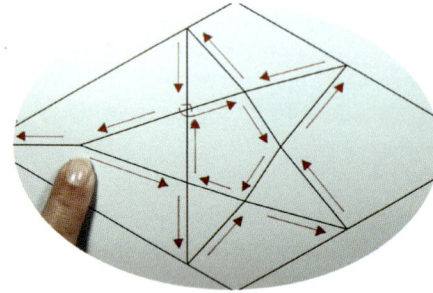

If you like puzzles you can plan your route to have as much continuous sewing as possible, like with this star, which can be sewn continuously with one long thread.

No matter what sewing sequence you use, you can avoid confusion by placing your stitched pieces down *wrong side up* in the proper position when you pick up the next piece.

At the end of every seam, before you cut your thread, lay the pieces down *wrong side up* to see if the next piece can be added continuously, as demonstrated in the DVD lesson.

mirror image

Since freezer paper templates are ironed onto the wrong side of the fabric, they always produce the mirror image.

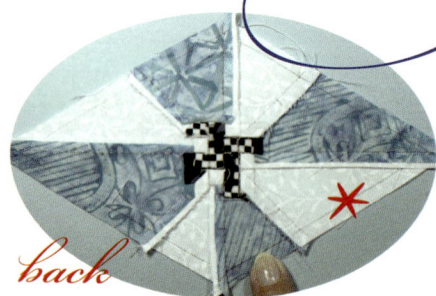

Mirror image means that the placement of fabrics on the back is the opposite of what is on the front. This is always the case, but most of the diamonds are symmetrical, so we do not notice it, but...

...for diamonds like these that are not the same on the left and the right sides, you may want to take mirror image into consideration. Compare the front and back of other turquoise diamonds on the pattern pages, like #2 and #3.

TWO TIPS: Print the patterns from the optional *QD2 CD*, with the "mirror image" option set on your inkjet printer—and *always* pick up the next piece to be stitched with all of the pieces *wrong side up*—as demonstrated in the DVD lesson.

Quilted Diamonds 2

Remove the freezer paper just before you are ready to stitch two pieces together. Some quilters like to leave the paper on, but I prefer to hold fabric, rather than paper, while I stitch. Use the crosshairs to re-mark lines, if necessary.

You can use an extra needle as a pin. I have never found pins that are finer than the #12 sharps I use, so I have 2 or 3 needles stuck into my sewing surface to be used interchangeably as pins or needles.

Align two pieces, right sides together, and pin at the first matching point, which is often the crosshair at the end of the seam. Pin as you go, one match at a time. Extra pins can catch your thread.

running stitch

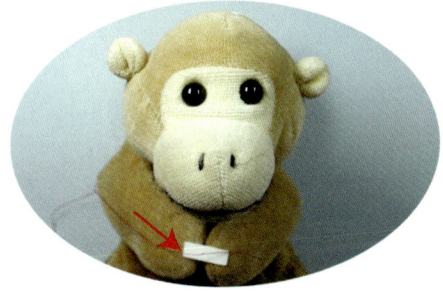

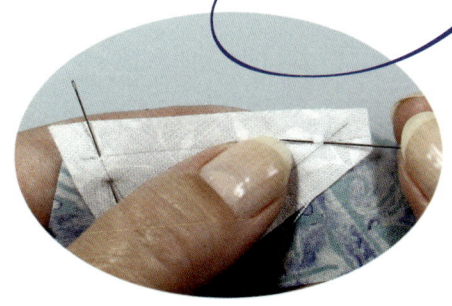

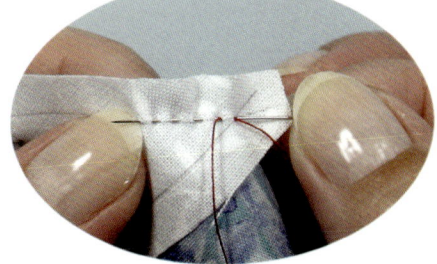

Try using a very small quilter's knot and a backstitch to start a seam. The quilter's knot is demonstrated on the DVD. I love pinning and stitching these small seams!

To start, hold the needle straight down, push it through the crosshairs at right angles to the fabric, and bring it up about 1/16 of an inch away on the seam line.

Then, go down through the crosshairs again, and back over the same stitch (called a backstitch or locking stitch) and load 3 to 5 more stitches.

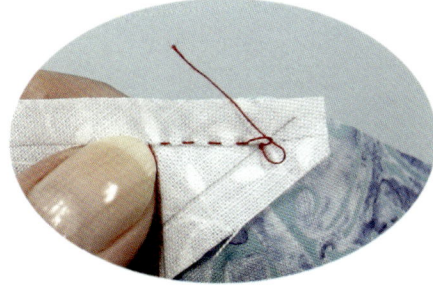

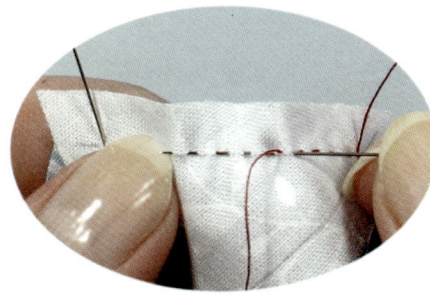

Catch the tail of the thread under one of the first stitches if you can, and continue with a simple running stitch.

Each time you load, insert the needle behind the last stitch you made, to make a backstitch. This gives added stability to the seam.

Load 3 to 5 stitches at a time, and check the underside to be sure the stitching line is straight before pulling the needle through.

running stitch

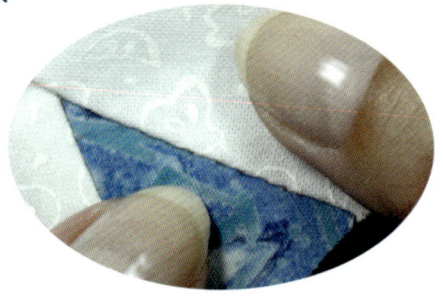

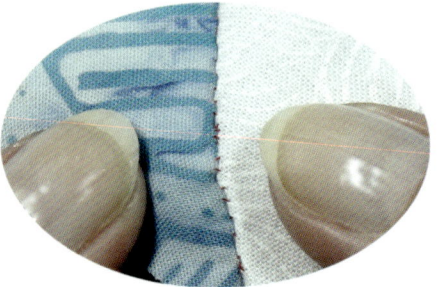

I like to pull firmly and then smooth the seam before loading the needle again.

There must be enough tension on the thread so the stitches do not show on the front, but not so much that the seam puckers.

If the thread is too loose, the seam will separate and your stitches will show in the seam on the front.

seam endings

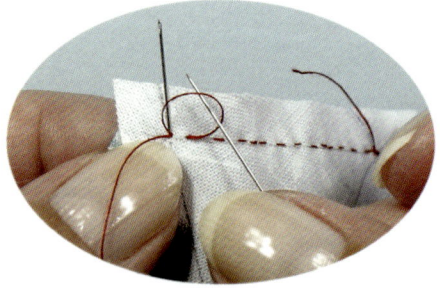

You will end each seam at the crosshair. Adjust the size of the last stitch before the end of the seam to be sure you are matching the crosshairs precisely...

... and then backstitch. Unlike machine pieced seams, hand pieced seams begin and end at the seam allowance, and this has advantages for pressing and trimming!

You can cut the thread now, leaving a 1-inch tail, and catching it under the last loop, but before you cut, look to see if the next piece can be added *continuously*, just by turning a corner.

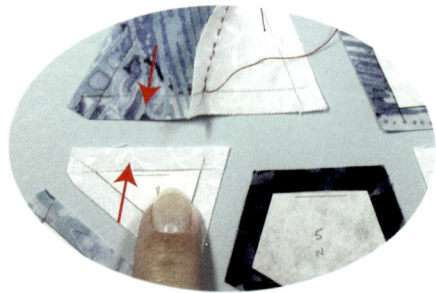

To stitch continuously, pick up the next piece with all the pieces *wrong side up*. Place right sides together, and begin the next seam just as before, with a backstitch.

There is no need to press before beginning the next seam. Pass the needle through crosshairs to get to the new seam, if necessary, with both hands working together.

Ideally, you will make 8 to 10 even stitches per inch, with a backstitch about every half inch, and the stitches will look the same on the front and the back.

1/4 inch seams

Learning to sew a scant ¼ inch seam will improve all of your quilting, whether by hand or by machine. On the DVD, Monkey wore his NASA space suit to remind you that this is not rocket science! It just takes a little practice.

It is a good idea to make a simple test diamond, like this, and learn ¼ inch seams allowances—*exactly of the true size for rational happiness.*[12] A *scant* ¼ inch seam allows for the turn of the fabric when the diamond is pressed.

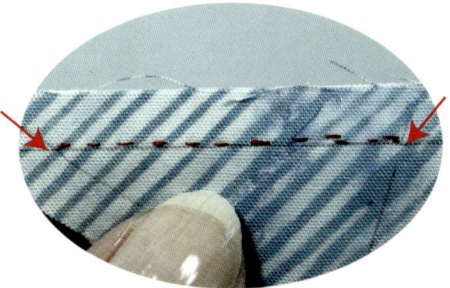

Use the crosshairs at each end, but in between, your stitches should lie on the outside edge of the seam line.

Check the finished size of each diamond against this template and adjust the size of your seam allowances, if necessary.

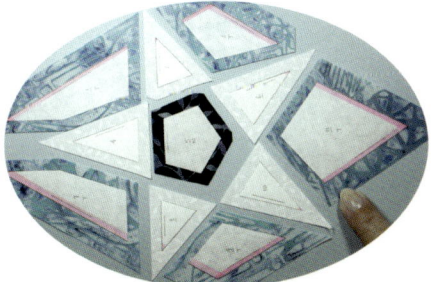

Some quilters cut ½ inch seam allowances on the outside edges. I don't use this method, but many quilters do, and you should decide for yourself. See the DVD for an example using ½ inch seam allowances on the outside edges.

unfinished size

finished size

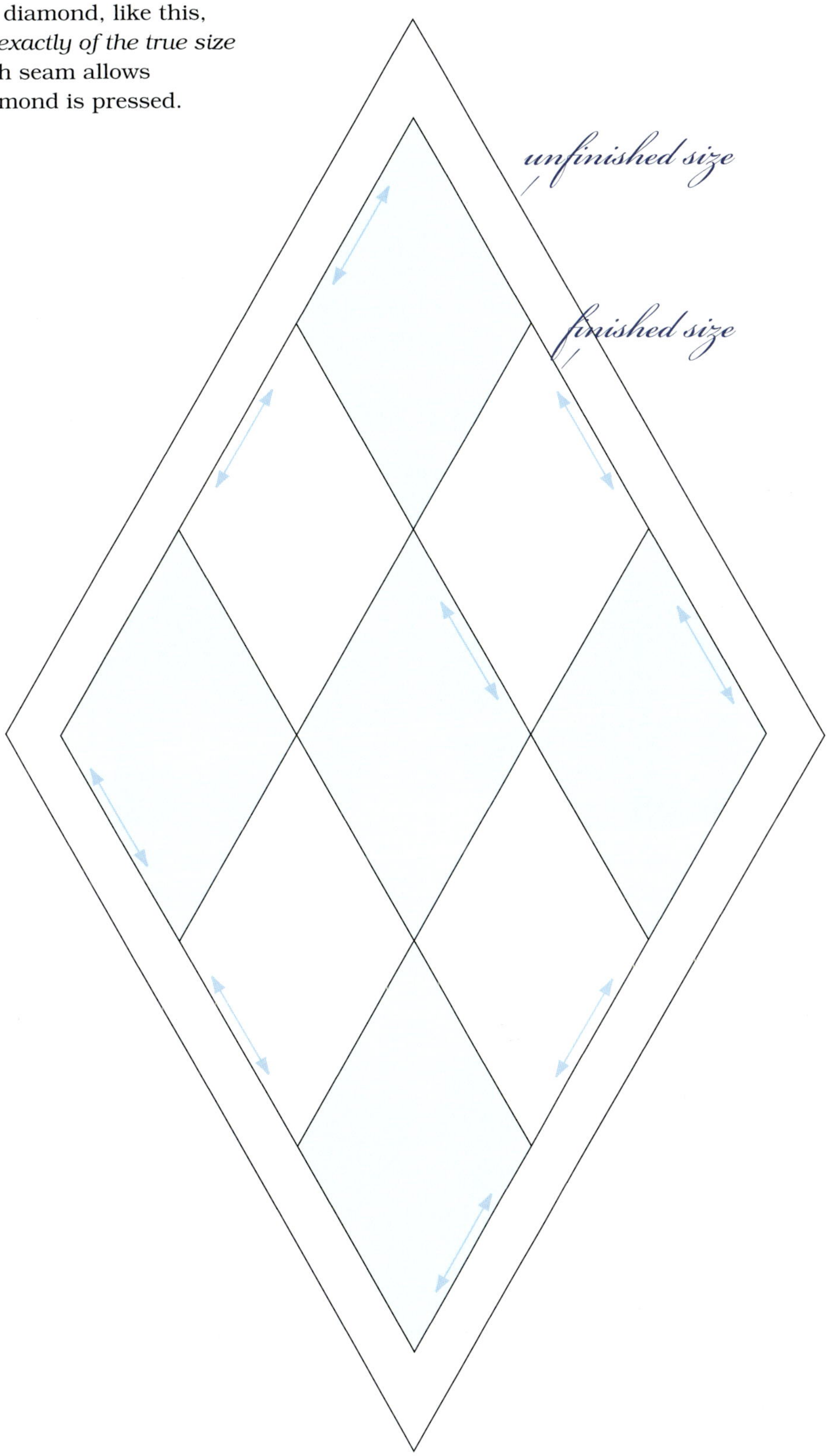

crossing seams

Pass the needle through crossing seam allowances, making a backstitch on each side of the intersection.

  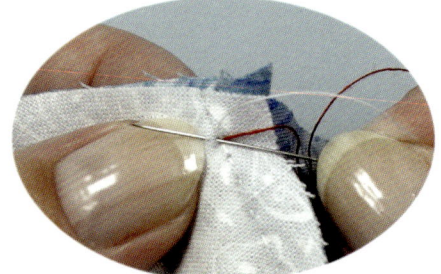

Hold the crossing seam allowances away from the needle until you get to the exact matching point and make your backstitch.

Pass the needle through the crossing seam allowances in the crosshairs. Never stitch through more than two layers of fabric.

Hold the crossing seam allowance out of your way and take a single stitch on the other side of the intersection, through the crosshair. Backstitch and continue along the seam.

inset seams

An inset seam is required when a piece is to be stitched into an angle formed by other pieces. It is sometimes called a Y seam. On the sewing machine, insets are tricky because we must stop stitching exactly ¼ inch from the end of the seam. That is what hand piecers do anyway, so they are as easy as ordinary straight seams for us.

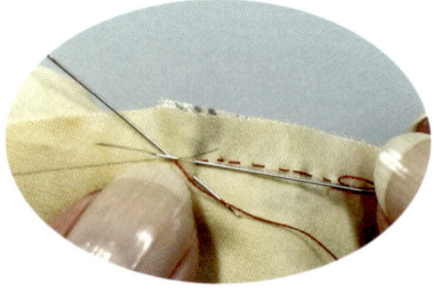  

For an inset, stitch from crosshair to crosshair for the first seam, as usual, ending with a backstitch. Do not cut the thread.

Pivot at the crosshair, pass the needle through the crossing seam allowance (if there is one), and pin the next section.

Take a single stitch and backstitch before continuing along the seam. This is just like an ordinary straight seam.

  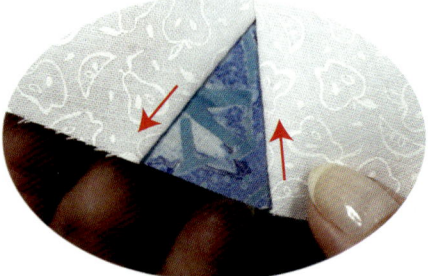

Continuous seams often look odd until you pivot, but if you always pick up the pieces the same way, *with the wrong side facing you*, you will learn to trust that it will all fit together.

Inset seams are so easy, you may decide to make them a habit. At the end of every seam, before you cut the thread, consider whether the next piece can be joined continuously.

I always look for opportunities for continuous stitching—whenever pieces join at an angle. For more examples of continuous stitching, see the DVD lesson. Select "inset seams."

many seams converging

There can be a tendency to get a bulge when many seams converge. With a few very minor adjustments, your diamonds will lie flat.

crosshair

On very sharp points, the crosshair is too far beyond the end of the freezer paper. Add a third line at the edge of the freezer paper. It is a better guide for the seam ending. When you gain experience, you can make this little adjustment without bothering to mark the third line.

Stitch *on* the seam line about an inch before and after the intersection when joining the last seam, and "circle the intersection" by passing the needle through all of the crosshairs, as on the DVD. You will have tight intersections and the points will match!

The seams will press well in a radiating manner (clockwise or counterclockwise), so that your trimmed diamond will lie flat and be easier to quilt.

curves

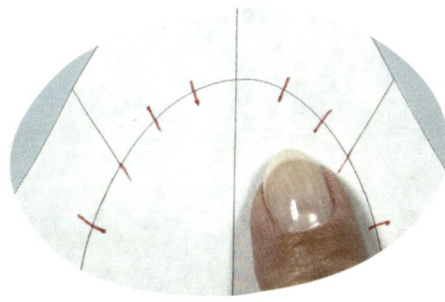

Before you cut the freezer paper pattern apart, mark matches along the curves. Matches should be closer together on tight curves.

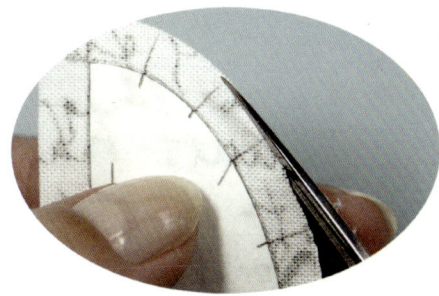

Cut the curves with scissors, eyeballing the ¼ inch seam. You may find curves easier to stitch if the seam allowance is slightly narrower than ¼ inch.

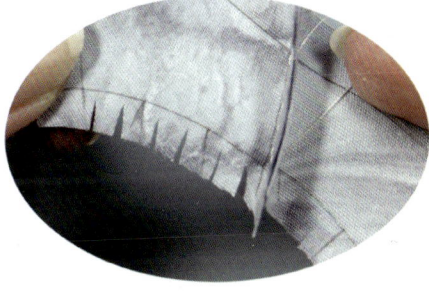

Clip the concave seam allowance, stopping a thread or two before the line. It is best to clip *between* the matching marks, rather than *at* the matching marks, so you have something to ease when you pin.

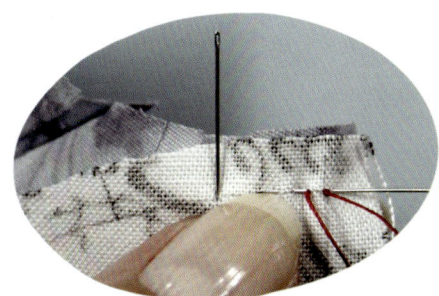

Just like all of my seams, I pin one match at a time. Extra pins can scratch my hand and catch the thread. You can stitch with the unclipped seam up, facing you, or...

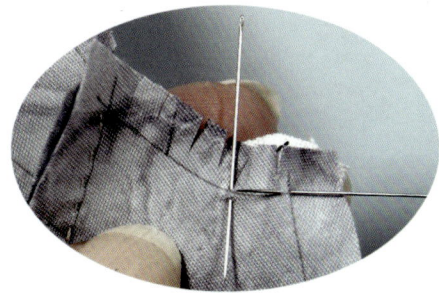

with the clipped seam up, facing you. It is just a matter of personal preference. Slow down, just taking 1 or 2 stitches at a time and backstitching every ½ inch or so.

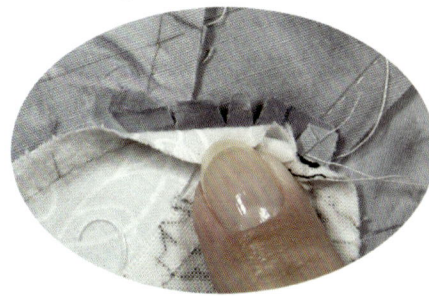

Curves will press well with the unclipped seam allowance pressed flat and the clips lying open in little v's underneath.

pressing

Monkey looks a little bit overwhelmed here, but every diamond is photographed from the back, so you have one example of pressing for each pattern in the book. Remember, that doesn't mean it is the only way! There are usually several different ways to press that would be equally good.

Monkey says, "Don't be intimidated by pressing." Since we do not sew through seam allowances, we do not have to press as we go and we have more options than machine piecers. Some pressing strategies make the diamonds look their best and reduce the bulk—and that makes the quilting easier!

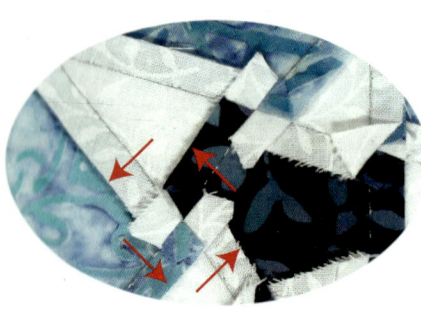

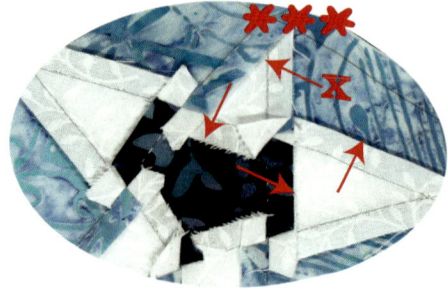

My first choice is always to press in a radiating manner around the intersections. It distributes the bulk well. It is only possible because we stitch just between the crosshairs.

Once the seams are pressed around one * intersection, they are committed for the adjacent intersection **...

...and to continue in a radiating manner with x sometimes results in too much bulk at sharp points *** so pressing in a radiating manner is not always possible.

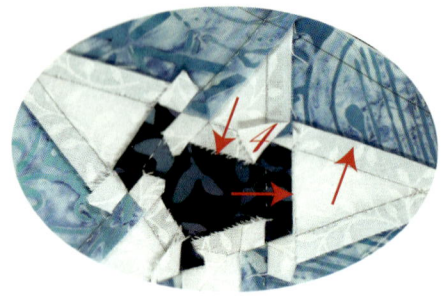

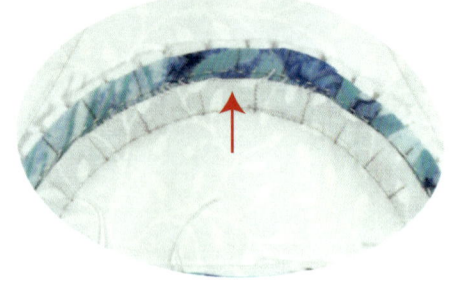

There are often other good choices. Sometimes you can make 3 seams radiate and fold the fourth back on itself (above). Don't forget, pressing in a radiating manner works for 3, 6 or 8 seam allowances too!

It is not necessary to press to the dark, the normal preference for machine piecers. Hand pieced seams can easily be trimmed so the dark seam allowances will not "shadow through" on the front.

Curves want to press in one direction, with the little v's lying open, covered by the unclipped seam allowance.

Finger press, or lightly iron from the wrong side first, finishing on the right side. Use a cotton setting with no steam. Lift and lower to avoid distorting your diamonds. A very small iron is big enough.

You might like to use a pressing roll to press some seams without affecting others. Avoid pressing seams open because it can allow fibers from the quilt batt to poke through. It should only be done very sparingly.

If worse comes to worst, just flatten everything with the iron from the right side, with the diamond lying on a towel—and eat chocolate to keep up your strength.

trimming

before

Trimming has at least two big advantages. It eliminates shadowing and reduces the bulk. That makes a diamond look its best and it makes the hand quilting easier!

after

I trim a scant 1/8 inch from each *dark* seam allowance. This is similar to "grading" in clothing construction. It makes the quilting easier.

yes   no

I do not recommend trimming both seam allowances. It feels lumpy compared to the graded seam and might allow the darker fabric to shadow through on the front.

Hand pieced seams are easy to trim because they are not sewn down, the way they are when machine pieced. Every seam allowance is accessible. Just unfold each one to trim.

Trim off any "dog ears" and other extra bits. You may lose some tails of thread in the process but don't worry about it.

If you save the trimmings, you will be amazed at the amount of weight you remove from your quilt top.

using electric quilt

print the patterns,

color the diamonds,

preview with fabrics,

simplify the designs,

& resize the patterns

The optional *Quilted Diamonds 2 CD* is attached here, if it is included with this copy of the book. It contains all the patterns in this book.

CD patterns in EQ format

Electric Quilt (EQ4 or EQ5) is required to open the project files.

Quilted Diamonds 2
more Austen-tatious diamonds to hand piece

©Linda Franz 2004 All rights reserved.
Please do not make illegal copies.

ISBN 0-9730304-3-7
Not for sale without the book.
www.lindafranz.com

Please see page 130 for CD installation instructions.

There is also an optional CD with the patterns from my first book, *Quilted Diamonds: Jane Austen, Jane Stickle & Friends*.

Available from
www.lindafranz.com

With the optional *Quilted Diamonds CDs* and Electric Quilt you can have all of the advantages of computer technology for your hand piecing.

The demonstration of EQ on the DVD is not a lesson, but is intended to show you that printing and coloring the diamonds on the *QD2 CD* can be an easy introduction to the software. EQ is very user-friendly.

You will be able to use many features of EQ as a beginner, but you will never outgrow EQ software. Several good books have been written about the more advanced features. There is always something new to learn.

EQ *Sketchbook*

When you first open a diamond file in the EQ Sketchbook, you will see that all of the blocks are square. *This is quite shocking!*[13] Don't worry!

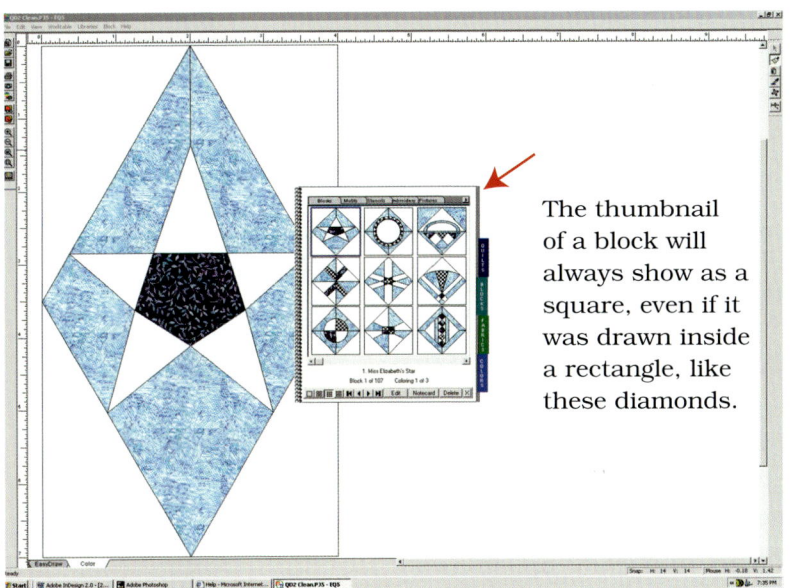

The thumbnail of a block will always show as a square, even if it was drawn inside a rectangle, like these diamonds.

In Jane Austen's day, the equivalent of a Palm Pilot personal organizer was *"a little bit of ivory, two inches wide."* [14]

Ladies penciled their shopping lists and other notes on tiny ivory tablets, which could be erased with a damp cloth.

Nevertheless, I have looked to Jane Austen for advice about the *QD2* EQ-compatible CD, and I think she would recommend it.

To work with one of the diamonds, you will need to get it out of the Sketchbook and onto the worktable. (See the instructions on page 130 to copy the project files onto your computer.)

1. Click the View Sketchbook button (or F8—a neat shortcut to learn).

2. Click the Blocks tab on the right edge of the Sketchbook.

3. Click on the block you want, which will then be outlined.

4. Click the Edit button at the bottom of the Sketchbook.

The block you selected will be on the worktable.

drawing board setup

To view it in the diamond shape, click Block > Drawing Board Setup, and set the block size to 4 x 7 inches. Voilà!

To draw diamonds in EQ, you should be familiar with all of the basic tools. However, *in excellent spirits, with fresh hopes and fresh schemes,*[15] diamonds might be just the thing to motivate you to become more familiar with this software.

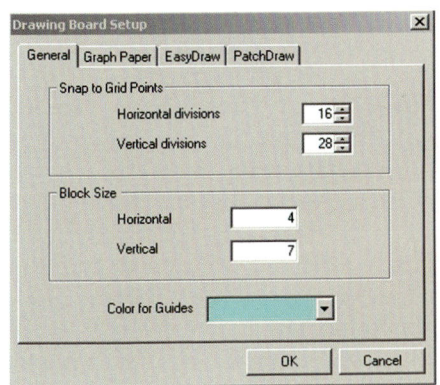

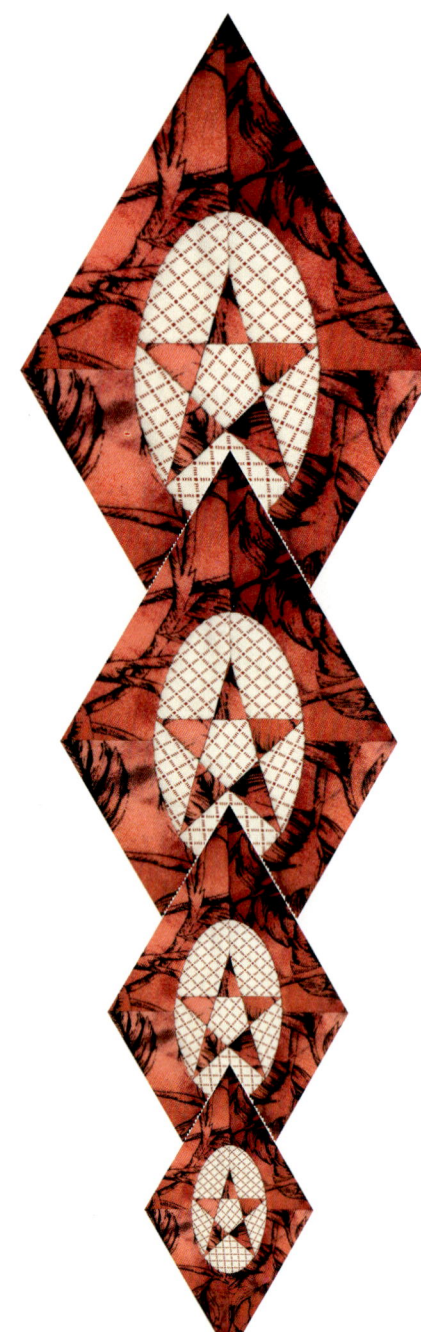

resizing the diamonds

The diamonds in *Quilted Diamonds 2: more Austen-tatious diamonds to hand piece* are 4 x 7 inches. Sixty-degree diamonds always have a ratio of width to height of 2 to 3.5.

With the *QD2 CD*, you may decide to print diamonds in other sizes, as long as you maintain this ratio. Some examples are:

width (inches)	height (inches)
1.43	2.5
2	3.5
2.63	4.5
3	5.25
3.88	6.75
4	7
5	8.75
5.71	10
6	10.5
6.86	12

It is not hard to print the diamonds *exactly of the true size for rational happiness.*[16] To calculate another size, decide on the desired width or height and use the appropriate formula:

1. If you know the desired width:

Multiply Desired Width by 3.5, then divide by 2 to get Required Height. E.g. If you want your diamonds to finish 2.5 inches wide,

2.5 x 3.5 = 8.75, then 8.75 ÷ 2 = 4.375 (round to 4.38 to print from EQ), so the diamonds are 2.5 by 4.38 inches.

2. If you know the desired height:

Multiply Desired Height by 2, then divide by 3.5 to get Required Width. E.g. If you want your diamonds to finish 5 inches high,

5 x 2 = 10, then 10 ÷ 3.5 = 2.857 (round to 2.86 to print from EQ), so the diamonds are 2.86 by 5 inches.

printing on freezer paper

Freezer paper templates can be used over and over. It is easy to see through freezer paper to trace, but you can also print on freezer paper with an inkjet printer. A laser printer is too hot for freezer paper!

I use an old rotary cutter to cut 18-inch wide freezer paper into rolls 4½ inches wide, for working with diamonds. I place the ruler on the plastic coated side of the freezer paper, so it does not slide around.

To print on freezer paper with EQ, I cut off about 10 inches of freezer paper, 18 inches wide, and slice it three times to get four pieces 4½ x 10. I print a diamond 4 x 7 inches on ordinary paper, to show me where to position the freezer paper on the page and then I run a hot, dry iron across the leading edge of the freezer paper and run the page through the printer a second time. This produces a perfect pattern, and the freezer paper peels off the other page neatly.

COLOR:

I usually just print the outline drawing but you might like to print in color. When you iron freezer paper onto white fabric, the edge can be hard to see so consider printing the pieces that will be white in pink or yellow. Otherwise, if you just print the outline you can use a highlighter to outline any pieces that don't show well on your fabric.

MIRROR IMAGE:

If there is a setting on your printer that allows you to print mirror image, you might like to use it and print your blocks in color. The "mirror image of the mirror image" is what you want in the finished diamond! (To counteract any new confusion, please see page 118.)

EXACT MEASUREMENTS:

Diamonds will not print in EQ without the outer rectangle (the four triangles). You will ignore the rectangle when you prepare your patterns, but it is a good idea to measure it to make sure that your printer is printing exactly 4 x 7 inches. I usually need to set my printer at 4 x 7.03 inches. Whenever you change the line width option, you should re-check the printed measurements, and adjust if necessary.

SHARPEST PRINTING OF OUTLINE:

File > Preferences > Print Quality set to 4. Then go to File > Print > Block and enter the width and height, which is 4 x 7 inches, or any other size you prefer, with the same ratio of width to height. Go to "Option" and change the line width, if desired, and click "print block name," if desired. The name will print backwards (see page 118) if you are using the "mirror image" setting of your inkjet printer.

FOR BEST PRINTING SHOWING FABRICS:

File > Preferences > Print Quality > Set Print Quality to 1 or 2. (Print Quality 4 will distort fabrics in an unsuitable way.) Go to File > Print > Block. Enter the block width and height, which is 4 x 7 inches, or any other size you prefer, with the same ratio of width to height. The option to print "showing fabrics" will not be available to you unless the block has been saved and shows in color in the print window. Click the arrows under the block in the print window to select the color version you want to print.

PAPER SAVING TIP:

I always select PREVIEW before printing and then click PRINT from the preview screen. That saves me from inadvertently printing in color when I mean to print the line drawing, or printing the wrong size.

editing and coloring diamonds

In the EQ Sketchbook, the thumbnail of a block will always show as a square. Set the drawing board to 4 x 7 inches, as described on page 127. To draw 60-degree diamonds in EQ, it is necessary to work inside a rectangle with a ratio of width to height of 2 to 3.5. Join the midpoints of the sides to get the outline of a diamond.

You can color the diamonds with the thousands of colors and fabrics provided in EQ, or you can scan your own fabrics onto your computer! Make an assessment before you buy fabric or spend a lot of time on a mix that doesn't work. This is a rational pleasure, and Jane Austen would approve.

In Electric Quilt, the diamonds are drawn within a rectangle, like this...

...and they are easy to set together in quilt layouts, with or without sashing. I used scans of my own fabric to preview my quilt.

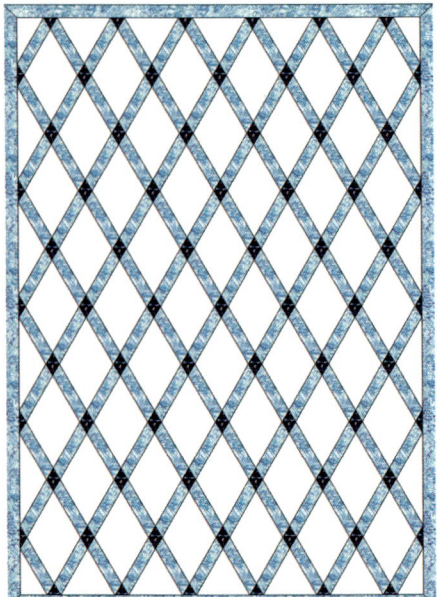

This "variable point layout" was created in EQ with spaces for 50 diamonds. (Layout is 6 blocks horizontal and 5 blocks vertical.) With 4 x 7 inch diamonds, 1-inch sashing and a 1-inch border, the program tells me it will finish 32 by 45.75 inches.

You will find helpful tips for working with Electric Quilt online. Please visit

www.electricquilt.com
www.lindafranz.com
(click on CD for EQ)

In addition to many resources on the EQ web site, there are online EQ courses at Quilt University, and www.planetpatchwork.com has a mail list called Info-EQ, which is devoted to discussion of Electric Quilt software. Members share ideas, ask questions, and provide assistance to other members. Representatives of Electric Quilt are often online to help. There are also challenges and other activities.

If you are new to EQ, promise yourself to take advantage of all the resources available to you.

You will never stop learning new things with this powerful software.

Designing quilt layouts in EQ is complicated by the fact that every diamond is part of a rectangle, but Electric Quilt is still helpful in designing quilt layouts like the ones on the following pages. They do not show the individual diamond designs, but they do create diamond spaces into which you can set diamonds. The setting blocks (diamond in a square, half star, etc.) are in their own project file on the optional *QD2 CD*.

Special Note: Be sure to check the "notecards" in the EQ Sketchbook for tips on drawing board size for stars, hexagons and triangles.

copy QD2 EQ *projects onto your hard drive:*

The *Quilted Diamonds 2 CD* contains all the diamonds in the book in both EQ4 and EQ5 format.

Put the *Quilted Diamonds 2 CD* in your CD drive.

Double-click on My Computer.

Double-click on the drive your CD is in. (It is the one with the picture of the drive and a little CD in front of it.)

Inside, you will see EQ4 and EQ5 project files.

> Click to select the EQ4 files if you use EQ4.
> Click to select the EQ5 files if you use EQ5.

On the EDIT menu, click Copy.

Now you need to paste them into a folder on your hard drive.

If you are using EQ4, go to C:\EQ4\pj4 or the location of your project files folder, if you changed the installation path of EQ4.

If you are using EQ5, go to C:\My Documents\My EQ5\pj5 or the location of your project files folder, if you changed the installation path of EQ5.

Create a new folder by clicking FILE menu, point to New and click Folder.

Rename this new folder "Quilted Diamonds 2" or whatever you like.

Double-click to open the new *Quilted Diamonds 2* folder.

On the EDIT menu, click Paste. The project files will appear in this new folder.

Double-click on your EQ (4 or 5) desktop icon to start the program.

Click the Open an Existing Project tab.

Click the little yellow folder at the bottom, marked "Click here to open a project not listed above."

Browse to the C:\EQ4\pj4\Quilted Diamonds or C:\My Documents\My EQ5\pj5\Quilted Diamonds folder (depending on your version of EQ).

Click on the *Quilted Diamonds 2* project.

Click Open.

You can then print off the patterns in the size you need or start coloring!

If you would like the *Quilted Diamonds 2* blocks to be accessible from every project you create in EQ, you can copy them into your block libraries, using the instructions in the Design Cookbook.
EQ4 Design Cookbook: p. 56-57
EQ5 Design Cookbook: p. 134-135

designing settings

I enjoy designing with freezer paper templates. There are some great ideas and tips on the next few pages, but if you are in a hurry, here it is in a nutshell: draw the finished size on freezer paper and add the seam allowances when you are cutting the fabric. All you need is a pencil and a ruler—but designing in EQ is fascinating!

My working method is to sew *a considerable hoard of diamonds*[17] and then think about how to set them.

I have never planned a quilt and known how it would look in advance. Luckily, freezer paper templates allow that kind of flexibility.

When I designed Love & Friendship (page 6), I made all of the diamonds and assembled the quilt top *before* I designed the center medallion. I had a quilt top with a huge diamond hole in the middle. This is not generally recommended but hand piecing with freezer paper templates is so precise you can get away with it!

I draw the pattern on freezer paper in the finished size and add the seam allowances when I cut the fabric. It is the same method whether I am designing a tiny diamond or fitting a design into the front of a blouse. See pages 140 and 141.

In these pages, there are ideas for setting your diamonds. These ideas are on the optional *QD2 CD* but they are also simple to draw with a pencil and paper. You will also find a chapter on settings in my first book—plus quilting designs and scalloped bindings.

I sometimes use three diamonds in a half star on the front of my blouses. There are many ways to design settings based on a half star. They are especially nice for borders, and whole stars have been favorites with quilters for years. See pages 134, 135, 140 and 141.

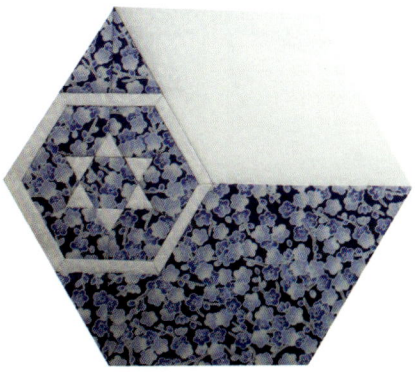

Baby blocks are a great way to create illusions with color. The setting for three diamonds in a hexagon is rectangular. See pages 136 and 137.

By setting the diamond on the diagonal inside a square, you can have the best of both diamonds and squares. The effect can be similar to sashing.

Quilters tend to be more comfortable working with squares and it opens up unlimited opportunities for settings, lined up in straight rows or on point, with or without sashing. See pages 132 and 133.

Three diamonds can be set into a triangle. This set makes some surprising secondary designs possible too. See pages 138 and 139.

diamond in a square

Drawing the right size square for any size diamond is easy, using a paper folding method. You can set any size diamond on the diagonal of a square this way.

For diamonds that are 4 x 7 inches, like the ones in *Quilted Diamonds* and *Quilted Diamonds 2*, your square will be 4.95 x 4.95 inches—just a smidgen less than 5 inches. (The magic formula is: 7 ÷ 1.414 = 4.95)

The diamond in a square is also ready and waiting for you on the *QD2 CD* to use in settings like the ones shown here or to print in any size.

You may *proceed to examine this mystery,*[18] and use Euclidean geometry to calculate the sides of a square from the length of the diagonal by monkeying around with the square or square root of the hypotenuse and multiplying or dividing by π, or similar. If your eyes glaze over as soon as you notice X and Y on a diagram, you can get the same results by folding freezer paper. (Be a mathematical prodigy: x ÷ 1.414 = y.)

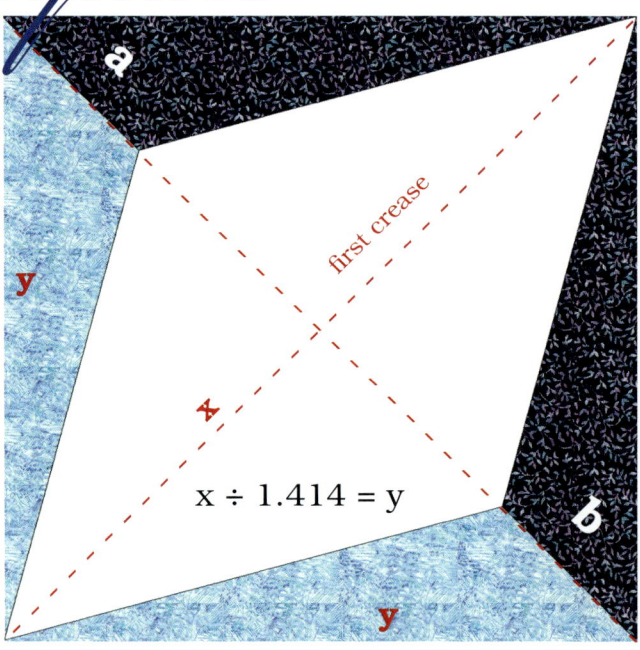

$$x \div 1.414 = y$$

Use the formula for x and y—OR fold paper to make a template for setting a diamond (any size) in a square:

1. Start with the outline of your diamond (for tracing) and a piece of freezer paper larger than you expect your block to be. (It must have 90° corners.)

2. Fold the bottom edge to meet the side edge to get a diagonal crease in the paper, as shown above. (Crease is 45°.) Open it out.

3. Trace the outline of any diamond, any size, with the vertical center of the diamond along the crease, as shown above.

4. Fold the tracing of the diamond in half, to get a crease at right angles to the first one.

I designed this quilt in EQ5 with 16 white spaces for diamonds. You might like to choose 16 diamonds from one novel (see the index) or choose 16 stars, 16 baskets, or any other favorites.

EQ calculates the finished size as 25 x 25 inches, with sixteen 4 x 7 inch diamonds, 1-inch sashing and 1-inch borders. The same layout in a quilt 97 x 97 inches would require 256 diamonds. Monkey says that would save you the trouble of choosing which *QD2* designs to leave out and allow you to include some of the designs from *Quilted Diamonds* (my first book) too.

5. With the page still folded as in step 4, cut the other two sides of the square, using the edge of the paper as a guide.

6. Open the fold and use a ruler to draw two short seam lines from the side points of the diamond to the corners, along the second crease, as **a** and **b** above.

If you know the size of square you want to use, you can work backwards to determine the size of the diamond.

x = 1.414y

For example, an 8 inch square will have a diamond that is 11.3 inches high, and you can calculate the width using the formula on page 128.

The square is a good way to frame diamonds of inconsistent size if you are swapping with friends.

Replace the diamond-shaped white spaces with your favorite *QD2* designs.

These diamond-in-a-square quilt layouts are on the *QD2 CD* but you can draw the old-fashioned way too.

half stars & stars

Stars are a sparkling way to set diamonds. Once you have the template drawn on freezer paper you will find many ways to use them. Half stars are very effective in borders and I use them on my blouses.

For 60-degree diamonds that are 4 x 7 inches, like the ones in *Quilted Diamonds* and *Quilted Diamonds 2*, the rectangle is 7 x 12 inches. If that is your size you can ignore the instructions here, and just trace your diamonds in the position shown in the diagram.

A half star in a rectangle block is also on the *QD2 CD* to use in settings like the ones shown here or to print in any size. Your drawing board setup and print size can be anything in a ratio of 12 to 7. (This is noted in the EQ Sketchbook on the Notecard.)

There is some fascinating geometry in 60-degree diamonds. The width of the diamond always equals the length of each of the four sides. You might find it easier to picture 60-degree diamonds as two equilateral triangles, or you may choose to ignore the entire question of **x** and **y** and, in the spirited voice of Catherine Morland, cry out, *"It is the horridest nonsense you can imagine,"*[19] and enjoy quilting with stars without any mathematics at all. (Mathematical friends will calculate the width of the rectangle using a formula 3x = y.)

I designed this quilt in EQ using the half star block. If you use your 18 favorite diamonds in the white spaces, the plain diamonds are a buffer (similar to sashing) between diamond designs.

The finished size is 38 x 30 inches using 4 x 7 inch diamonds and one-inch borders. The same layout can be used with larger or smaller stars or more stars, of course, to make any size you need. You can play with additional borders and variations in Electric Quilt.

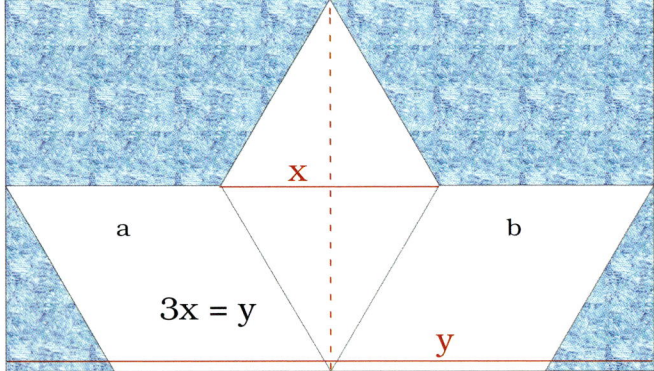

Use the formula for x and y—OR fold paper to make a template for setting three diamonds (any size) in a half star in a rectangle:

1. Start with the outline of your diamond (for tracing) and a piece of freezer paper wider than you expect your block to be (shortcut: y = 3 times x) and the height of your diamonds. (It must have 90° corners.)

2. Fold the paper in half both ways and make sharp creases. Open it out.

3. Trace the outside edge of your diamond, any size, with the vertical center of the diamond along the crease, indicated by the dotted red line, above.

4. Trace the outline of your diamond for the two side diamonds, **a** and **b**. One edge will fall along the other crease.

5. To mark the outer edges of the rectangle, make a crease at each side to intersect the outer points of the side the diamonds **a** and **b**. Cut along those creases.

Now you can use the 4 blue shapes to set 3 diamonds.

The star looks quite different turned on its side.

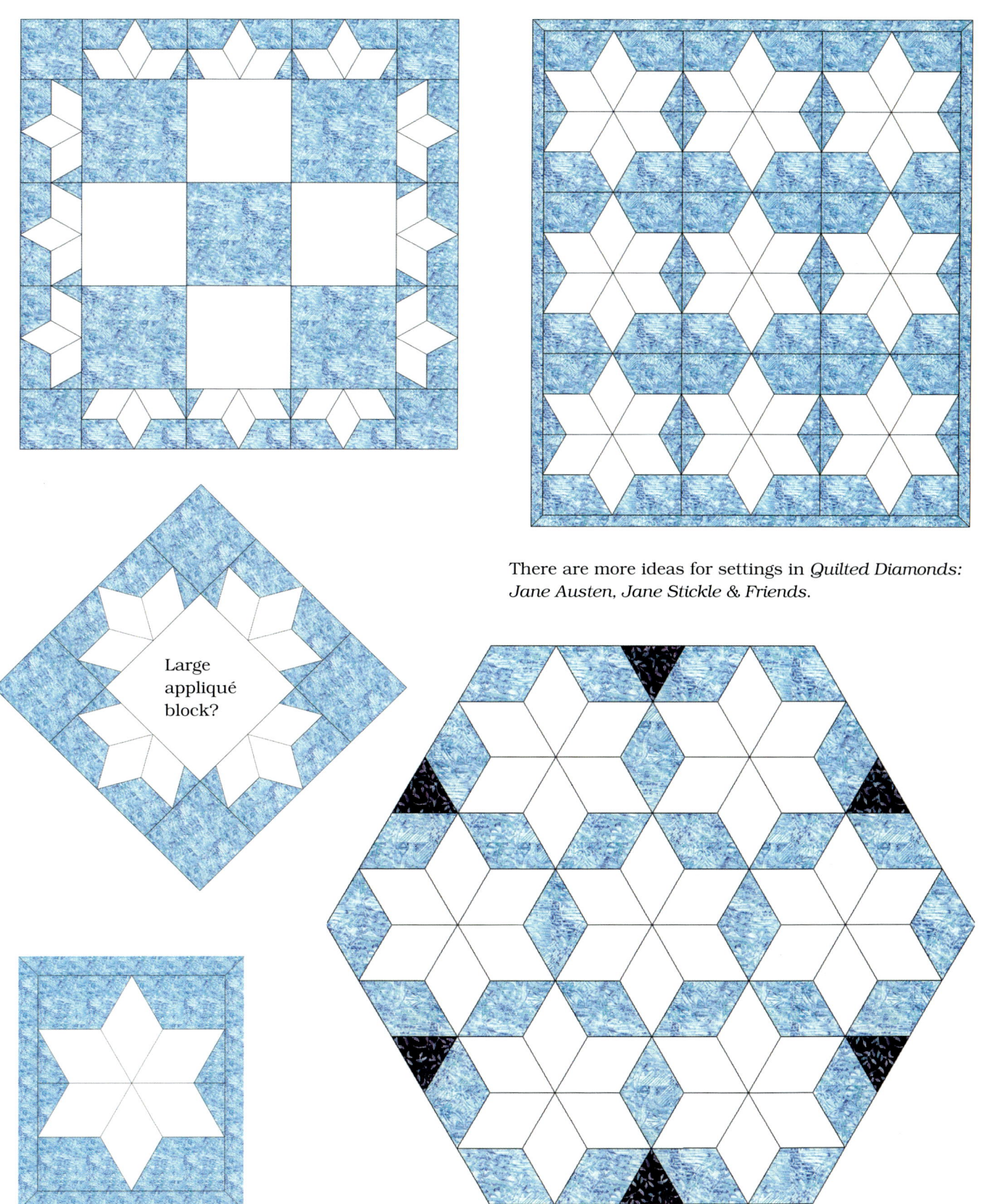

There are more ideas for settings in *Quilted Diamonds: Jane Austen, Jane Stickle & Friends.*

Large appliqué block?

Replace the diamond-shaped white spaces with your favorite *QD2* designs.

These quilt layouts are on the *QD2 CD*. The hexagon is the Seven Sisters block (not a quilt) in the project file.

hexagons

Once you have a hexagon template drawn on freezer paper you will find many ways to use it. Diamonds set as "baby blocks" can create optical illusions of depth, as in the quilts shown here.

For diamonds that are 4 x 7 inches, like the ones in *Quilted Diamonds* and *Quilted Diamonds 2*, three diamonds fit inside a rectangle that is 7 x 8 inches. If that is your size you can ignore the instructions here and just trace your diamonds into position, as shown.

The hexagon in a rectangle is also on the *QD2 CD* to use in settings like the ones shown here or to print in any size. Your drawing board setup can be anything in a ratio of 7 to 8. (This is noted in the EQ Sketchbook on the Notecard.)

Hexagons are closely related to half stars, geometrically speaking. There is some fascinating geometry in hexagons which you may have studied in school. I hope that **x** and **y** will not interfere with your enjoyment of this setting. To paraphrase the teenaged Jane Austen[20] "I will save you the task of reading again what you have read before, and myself the trouble of writing what I do not perfectly recollect, by giving paper folding instructions." (Okay, mathematical prodigies: 2x = y.)

I designed this quilt in EQ using the hexagon block set on point. If you set your 6 favorite diamonds in the white spaces, the plain diamonds are a buffer (similar to sashing) between diamond designs. Or, maybe replace the checkerboard diamonds with *QD2* diamonds in another color? The possibilities...oh, my!

The same layout can be used any size, of course, and you can play with additional borders and variations in Electric Quilt.

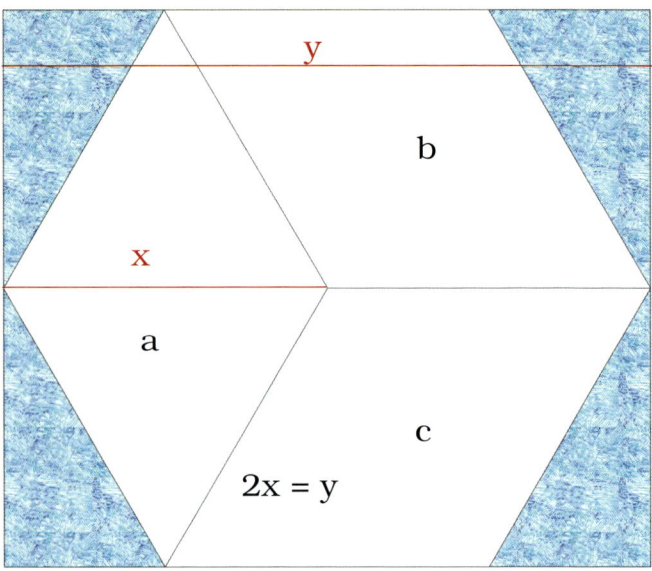

Use the formula for x and y—OR fold paper to make a template for setting three diamonds (any size) in a hexagon in a rectangle:

1. Start with the outline of your diamond (for tracing) and a piece of freezer paper the height of your diamond and twice as wide as your diamond. (It must have 90° corners.)

2. Fold the paper in half (bottom edge to top edge) and make a sharp crease to mark the center. Open it out.

3. Trace the outside edge of any diamond, any size, in position **a** above, with the horizontal center of the diamond along the crease and the left edge of the diamond even with the left edge of the paper.

4. Trace the outline of the two side diamonds, **b** and **c**.

Now you can use the 4 blue triangles to set any three diamonds as a hexagon in a rectangle.

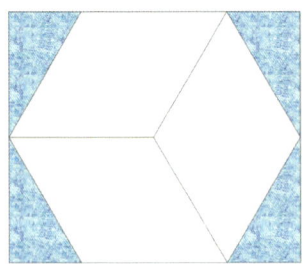
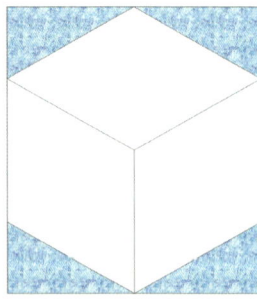

The hexagon looks quite different turned on its side.

Think of each of the diamond spaces as a facet in a sparkling gem to showcase your diamond designs.

Why not replace all of the plain diamonds with *QD2* diamonds in a different color for each position?

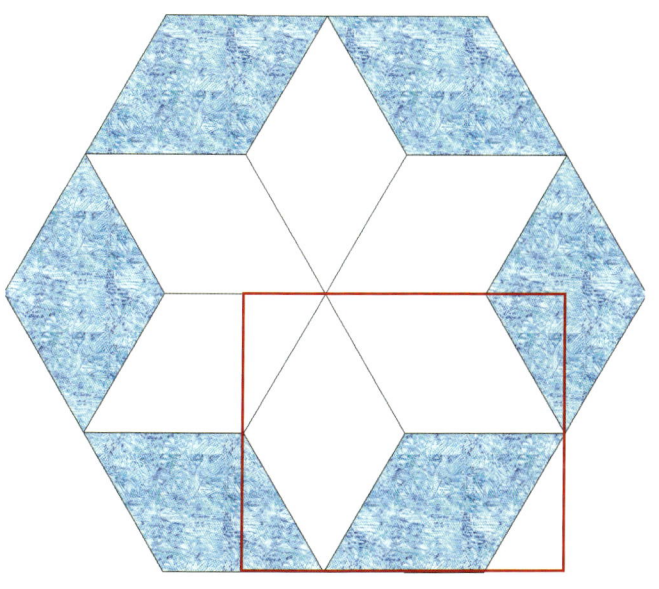

....and then you may want to ponder the relationship between hexagons and diamonds...in more stars!

triangles

Three diamonds fit nicely into triangles too. Claire Baker of Indiana set her diamonds this way and by alternating with plain setting triangles she created a secondary star design.

For diamonds that are 4 x 7 inches, like the ones in *Quilted Diamonds* and *Quilted Diamonds 2*, three diamonds fit inside a rectangle that is 10.5 x 12 inches. If that is your size you can ignore the instructions here, and just trace your diamonds into position on freezer paper, as shown.

The triangle (in a rectangle) is also on the *QD2 CD* to use in settings like the ones shown here or to print in any size. Your drawing board setup can be anything in a ratio of 10.5 to 12. (This is noted in the EQ Sketchbook on the Notecard.)

Each of the setting triangles is made up of three 60-degree diamonds and three 60-degree triangles. These triangles are called equilateral. Each diamond is also a combination of two equilateral triangles, so you can see the big equilateral triangle as nine equilateral triangles, or three equilateral triangles and a hexagon. Therefore, you can also create this triangle setting by adding three equilateral triangles to a hexagon of three diamonds (as on page 137). That is all I have to say about this. I am going to sit in a corner now (90-degrees) and think. (Okay, mathematicians: 1.5x = y. You probably knew that already.)

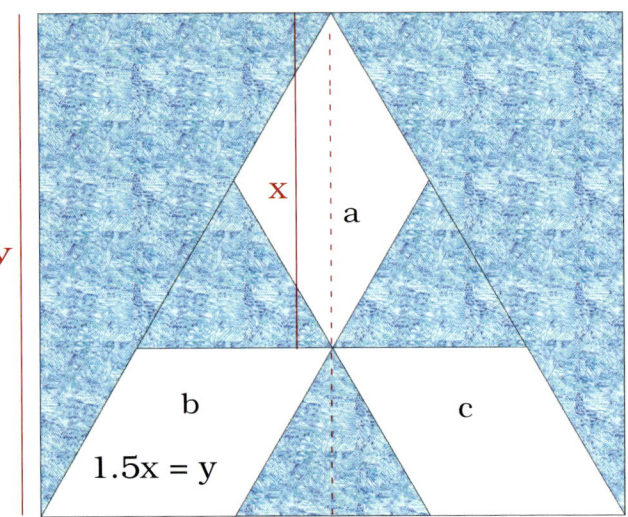

$1.5x = y$

Use the formula for x and y—OR fold paper to make a template for setting three diamonds (any size) in a hexagon in a rectangle:

1. Start with the outline of your diamond (for tracing) and a piece of freezer paper that is exactly 3 times wider than the width of your diamonds. (The paper must have 90° corners.)

2. Fold the paper in half (left edge to right edge) and make a sharp crease to mark the center, as indicated by the dotted red line. Open it out.

3. Trace the outside edge of any diamond, any size, in position **a** above, with the vertical center of the diamond along the crease (indicated by the dotted red line) and the top point of the diamond even with the top edge of the paper, as shown.

4. Trace the outline of the two side diamonds, **b** and **c**. One edge of each will fall along the edge of the paper and the points of all three diamonds will meet.

5. Use a ruler to extend the lines of diamond **a** to finish the sides of the triangle.

Now you can use the blue shapes as templates to set any three diamonds as a triangle in a rectangle. You will probably also want to make a plain setting triangle, the same size.

I designed this quilt in EQ, using the triangle in a rectangle. Use your favorite *QD* diamonds in the white spaces.

There are many variations on this setting which you can explore with EQ or using paper and pencil.

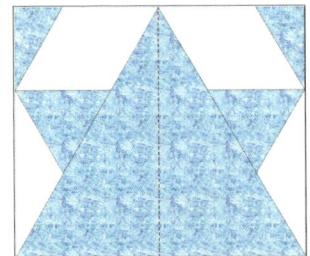

The triangle setting is on the *QD2 CD*, but because it can only be used in settings as a rectangle, there is also a split version of the triangle (left) which you may find helpful in planning your quilt layouts.

Quilted Diamonds 2

Jane in the Sky with Diamonds
(81 x 91 inches, detail)

Claire Baker of West Lafayette Indiana made 117 diamonds from *Quilted Diamonds: Jane Austen, Jane Stickle & Friends,* and set them as triangles with alternating pale blue setting triangles to get her star design. Claire's bright diamonds really sparkle in this setting.

Can you see the blue stars below? And the two hexagon shapes? One hexagon is half the size of the other.

Replace the diamond-shaped white spaces with your favorite *QD2* designs.

This quilt layout is on the *QD2 CD*. See the EQ Sketchbook Notecard for drawing board setup.

This setting has large spaces for beautiful quilting. There is a chapter in my first book with quilting designs for diamonds, and also more information on finishing your quilt with a scalloped binding—one of my favorites!

any shape you like

Using freezer paper templates, you can set your diamonds into any shape you like—even one with armholes.

When I am not in the mood for a big quilt project but want to have some stitching therapy, I choose three diamonds from *Quilted Diamonds 2* or *Quilted Diamonds* to coordinate for a blouse or for a little quilt to use on the front of a tote bag. I stitch the diamonds by hand and then finish with the sewing machine. Monkey is a hand piecing snob, but I still enjoy my sewing machine.

Any clothing pattern can become your setting for diamonds. I start with a commercial pattern and make adaptations to ensure that the finished garment will fit me *and* be easy to wash and press.

You might prefer to make jackets or vests instead of blouses, or to set the diamonds into sleeves. I have included some general tips that you can adapt to your own situation. These instructions assume you have some experience with clothing construction.

For a simple sleeveless top in my size, one yard of cotton fabric is enough for the front and back, bias binding and facings, and I add a few scraps of coordinating colors for the diamonds. Many of my quilt shop purchases come out of the clothing budget. It is a good justification for buying at least a yard!

1. Start with a commercial pattern that fits you. The features I like about the blouse pattern I use are:
♦ The neckline is just large enough to go over my head so there is no closure to consider when I design.
♦ The neckline & armholes have smooth curves so are suitable for double-fold bias binding (just like a quilt!) which eliminates the need for interfacing and makes a professional-looking finish.
♦ There are no darts to interfere with the patchwork design.
♦ Straight side seams allow me to use French seams, giving a professional finish and making the garment washable.

2. Trace the pattern front onto freezer paper, *without* the seam allowances (usually 5/8 inch on commercial patterns) for the finished size.

3. Draw the placement of the diamonds, as shown above. Extend lines to the side seams, armholes or neckline to allow it to be pieced.

4. Note the seam allowance on the edge of each piece for reference when cutting the fabric:
♦ armholes and neckline - No seam allowance, because I use binding, just like a quilt.
♦ shoulders and side seams - ½ inch is enough for narrow French seams on the side seams.
♦ interior seams - ¼ inch, like any quilt block.

5. Re-draw the front facing as in steps 2 and 4, so it will cover the pieced area of the blouse.

6. Mark grain line and label each piece. Add matches on the seams (see page 116).

The setting I use most often for diamonds is *not* a square, a rectangle, a hexagon or a triangle, but a custom designed blouse.

Monkey says you can never have enough totes. Add a quilted pocket to any tote bag.

The directions for Monkey's Ultrasuede tote are on my web site at *www.lindafranz.com*

A pullover top is a "blank canvas" for setting diamonds.

All three diamonds can match in the half star design.

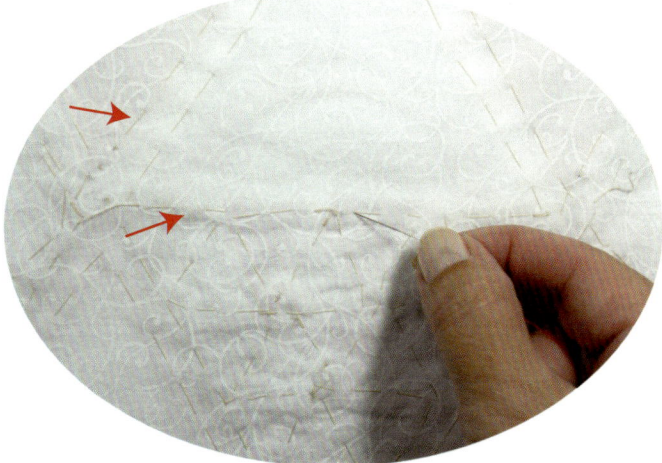

If I do not want to quilt the layers of the top, I will take large running stitches on the inside through the facing, catching all of the seam allowances, but not going through the front. It only takes a few minutes and it stabilizes the seam allowances for repeated washings.

Another little tip is to take a few hand stitches in the shoulder seam so the seam allowances will not bunch up when the blouse is washed. This also works to keep the facings in place at the side seams. When my tops come out of the dryer they just need a light pressing.

Mary Althaus
Sandy Arbuthnot
Annette Austin
Claire Baker
Anne Barney
Jane Billingsley
Tilde Binger
Linda Brandau
Val Champ
Laura Chaskes
Tracy Craven
Alice Curtis
Kate Donnelly
Karen Ehrhardt
Leah Estrin
Karan Flanscha
Linda Gerig
Tutu Haynes-Smart
Linda Hershfield
Vicki Hill
Shirley Homer
Sara Hougaard
DiAnn Hunter
Ingrid Jensen
Joni King
Susanne Kleen
Marcie Knudson
Mitzie Lepka
Jane Lindsay
Connie Lukacs
Connie Makl
Wenche Martinsen
April Mathis
Pam Matthews
Jeanne Meddaugh
Judy Meyer
Judy Miller
Goldie Morrow
Jane Newble
Mary Nudge
Virginia Ohr
Brenda Papadakis
Terri Petasek
Barbara Pyter
Becky Rieger
Debbie Russell
Deborah Schultz
Pat Sloan
Gail Stewart
Elaine Terdal
Cassandra Thoreson
Emily Undem
Sharyn Woerz
Judy Wright

I saved the best setting for last. Many online friends made this diamond quilt for me as a surprise.
The only difficulty...was in concealing the excess of her pleasure.[21]

It is a beautiful quilt, and it is even more precious because they collected an album of letters about
our friendships. It is a treasure to me. Emily Undem sent out invitations and spent two years getting
it all together. In that time Emily also had her first baby. Sharyn Woerz assembled the quilt top.

Quilted Diamonds 2

selected bibliography

Jane Austen's novels are widely available and all can be viewed in recent movies on DVD and VHS.

Sense and Sensibility (1811)
Pride and Prejudice (1813)
Mansfield Park (1814)
Emma (1816)
Northanger Abbey (1818)
Persuasion (1818)

Web sites:

The Republic of Pemberley
http://www.pemberley.com
The Jane Austen Society of North America
http://www.jasna.org

The Jane Austen Museum (Chawton)
http://www.janeaustenmuseum.org.uk
The Jane Austen Center in Bath
http://www.janeausten.co.uk

There are many excellent biographies of Jane Austen. These are just a few of my favorites:

Jane Austen's Letters, edited by Deirdre LeFaye. (Oxford University Press, 1995)
A Memoir of Jane Austen, J. E. Austen-Leigh. (1870, reprinted by The Folio Society, 1989)
A Portrait of Jane Austen, David Cecil. (Constable & Co. Ltd., 1978)
Jane Austen A Biography, Elizabeth Jenkins. (Victor Golancz Ltd., 1948)

footnotes for hand piecers

1. E Ch. 53 **2.** P&P Ch. 31 **3.** P&P Ch. 22 **4.** Letters, p. 203 **5.** Letters, p. 201 **6.** P&P Ch. 49 **7.** P&P Ch. 28 **8.** E Ch. 51 **9.** E Ch. 19 **10.** NA Ch. 2 **11.** E Ch. 42 **12.** NA Ch. 21 **13.** P&P Ch. 16 **14.** NA Biographical Notice **15.** NA Ch. 9 **16.** NA Ch. 21 **17.** NA Ch. 20 **18.** NA Ch. 20 **19.** NA Ch. 7 **20.** The History of England **21.** NA Ch. 14

about the author & publisher

Linda Franz is an award winning Canadian quilter. You may recognize her from Simply Quilts with Alex Anderson on HGTV. Her first hand pieced bed quilt won a first place ribbon at the AQS show in Paducah, among other awards.

Linda has taught in Canada and the US, including at the AQS show in Paducah Kentucky. She has enjoyed teaching hand piecing workshops for many guilds.

Linda has a BA in English Literature and graduated from the University of Toronto Law School with an LLB. Her first book, *Quilted Diamonds: Jane Austen, Jane Stickle & Friends* was also self-published and is available in quilt shops in the US, Europe, Australia and Canada.

Linda and her husband, Russell Bays, live in Burlington Ontario in the summer. Every autumn they load the car with fabric and Jane Austen's novels and head south to spend the winter in Naples Florida. For current contact information and more about Linda, please visit www.lindafranz.com

index

No promotional consideration has been received for
using any of the products in the book or in the DVD lesson.

Quilted Diamonds 2